CRITICISM

T0160186

CATHERINE BELSEY chaired the Centre for Critical
and Cultural Theory at Cardiff University before
moving to Swansea as Research Professor in English.
Much of her work is on Shakespeare and cultural
criticism. Her books include *Critical Practice* (1980,
second edition 2002), *Poststructuralism: A Very Short
Introduction* (2002) and *A Future for Criticism* (2011).

IDEAS IN PROFILE
SMALL INTRODUCTIONS TO BIG TOPICS

CRITICISM

CATHERINE BELSEY

P

PROFILE BOOKS

First published in Great Britain in 2016 by
PROFILE BOOKS LTD
29 Cloth Fair
London
EC1A 7JQ
www.profilebooks.com

A CIP catalogue record for this book is available from the British Library.

ISBN 978 1 78125 450 9
eISBN 978 1 78283 157 0

Designed by Jade Design
www.jadedesign.co.uk

Printed and bound in Great Britain by Clays Ltd, Elcograf S.p.A.

This book is dedicated with grateful thanks to the students of English at the University of Derby.

CONTENTS

1

THE PRACTICE OF CRITICISM

OPTIONS

'What do you think of it?'

Anyone who asks you this question is addressing you as a critic. Most of us practise criticism from time to time, if only at the level of choosing to see this movie, read that book or watch the other programme. The Sunday papers offer detailed critical coverage of current novels, plays, films and exhibitions. Reading groups and book clubs debate distinct critical reactions to the same work; literary festivals – more and more of them – thrive on critical discussions of new writing. Meanwhile, reading and talking about reading form part of the school curriculum from our earliest years. In consequence, critical habits are inculcated in childhood to the point where they come to seem natural or inevitable – for better or worse.

It's always possible to stop at 'I liked it' (or not) but the conversation stands a chance of advancing in interesting ways when we're more specific. This book is not a history of criticism, an encyclopaedia of famous critics or a dictionary of critical terms, but a reflection on criticism itself, the possibilities and options that confront casual readers, as well as reviewers, members of reading groups, students of

English and teachers of a discipline. How far do we make conscious choices about how and what we read (or view)? What do we conventionally look for in fiction? What might we look for?

Consideration of those issues will include some history, discussion of some famous critics and, indeed, some comments on critical terms. Over time, criticism has developed a vocabulary that singles out particular approaches to poetry and storytelling. The prevailing terminology is certainly worth our close attention but it might not be beyond improvement. Perhaps we could usefully expand the vocabulary we take for granted when we talk about reading (and viewing). There might be alternative questions that new terms would enable us to raise about reading in general or an individual work in particular.

Criticism does not confine itself to the analysis of plays, films, novels and poetry. All made objects are entitled to their own critics. Quite apart from the long and distinguished history of art criticism, there are music experts, not to mention restaurant reviewers and wine critics. Some of what I have to say applies to varying degrees in these fields too. But, while it includes marginally more about the visual field than, for example, viniculture, this book will focus primarily on fiction, and written fiction at that.

Why not come clean, then, and call it *literary criticism*? Because there is room for unease about the way *literary* divides the field in advance. Deliberately or not, the term implies a prior value judgement: *literature* is the good stuff, worth a particular kind of attention, and the rest is thought of at best as popular culture, at worst as pulp fiction or trash.

One problem with this distinction is that the judgement has usually been established in advance, in practice by the previous generation. Let's begin by taking nothing on trust.

The word *fiction* has its difficulties too, since it seems to stand as the opposite of fact. But poems, essays or memoirs may well lay claim to truth, while at the same time differentiating themselves from the particular kind of allegiance to fact asserted by history, science and social science. We have no comprehensive term for writing not primarily committed to relaying the facts. And *fiction* has the advantage of including cinema, opera and some kinds of painting.

The criticism of fiction has been practised in the West since ancient times – and debated for just as long. Aristotle, for example, took issue with Plato, who excluded fiction from his ideal republic. Aristotle wrote about tragedy in ways that still carry authority, but his views in turn have been contested: successive epochs have come back to the puzzling question he prompted of why tragedy gives pleasure. While subsequent criticism has embraced a range of activities, centring variously on themes or genres, on the formal construction of an individual work, or its place in history and in the specific history of fiction, all these approaches have given rise to debate.

But if nothing is finally settled, three main issues have preoccupied traditional criticism: judgement, morality and intention. Much effort has gone into constructing hierarchies of value: where, people have asked, does this individual work stand in the league table? Judgement often goes hand in hand with an insistence on the ethical value of the work. Is the pleasure we find in fiction best seen as sugar on a moral pill? Even pleasure itself has been thought suspect, a distraction from the serious task in hand. Meanwhile, can we make sense of the work without knowing who wrote it or what the author had in mind?

The attention paid to each of these critical priorities has varied in the course of time. Might the emphasis usefully change again in the future? Where has criticism come from – and where might it go? Most important of all, how can we best go about reflecting on these issues?

AN EXAMPLE

Criticism proceeds by putting forward answers to questions, and specific questions focus attention differently. They don't necessarily determine what we find. Instead, the work has an independent existence and may well surprise us. But looking for the moral truth of the work, say, is distinguishable from locating it in history, at least in the sense that it's possible to do one without the other; formal analysis is not the same as identifying the sources. Criticism includes all these options.

And now I too face a question: how best to begin to convey the variety of ways to advance the critical conversation beyond immediate likes and dislikes, tracing the emergence of the traditional critical preoccupations, and putting forward an alternative to them. The answer is probably to consider an example from different angles. The discussion will be more convincing if the example is available for inspection and, since there is probably no single work that everyone knows by heart, in practice that means reproducing it here. Not *King Lear*, then, or *Paradise Lost* or *War and Peace*. And preferably not a work so perplexing as to discourage on sight all but the most resolute. Ancient or modern? No single case can typify all possible instances. Whatever I choose will exclude certain concerns: impossible to reflect on verse forms if the text is in prose; pointless to look for narrative suspense in lyric verse.

The ideal example would be as self-contained as any structure of words ever can be. Not an excerpt, then. A *very* short story? A poem? Or perhaps both at once. Out of many possibilities, let's settle for this:

> A slumber did my spirit seal;
>   I had no human fears:
> She seemed a thing that could not feel
>   The touch of earthly years.
>
> No motion has she now, no force;
>   She neither hears nor sees,
> Rolled round in earth's diurnal course
>   With rocks and stones and trees.

Well, what *do* you think of it? Most people tend to like it at least enough to be prepared to give it some more thought. It's not threatening, they note: the vocabulary is simple enough; only one word has more than two syllables. It's clear, at least to an initial reading. And it invites us to care about the discovery it records, since the experience is one we might easily share, or be persuaded by the poem to imagine ourselves sharing.

And perhaps that's a good enough answer to the

question for now. As both reading groups and academic conferences sometimes reveal, strong investments, whether for or against, tend to generate fierce arguments. In the debates that follow, each side is ready to isolate those features that support its initial judgement, ignoring details that point another way, along with difficulties or complexities. Evaluation, so readily taken for granted as the first purpose of criticism, might in practice be its least helpful starting point. If we revert for a moment to wine critics, it's evident that the best of them don't just give grades to certain vintages. Instead, they try, against the odds, to convey in words something of the kind of flavour consumers might expect. True, this has its silly side ('a promiscuous little wine with a happy disposition') but at its best it can be illuminating. Something similar goes for criticism (which also has its silly side). The best criticism is generally more reflective than evaluative, more descriptive, eager to find a way to characterise the work.

Perhaps, in other words, we might shift the common question on its axis a little to open up more options. 'What do you think *about* it?' Or even just 'What do you think?'; 'What does the work prompt you to think?'

Before I dwell on the details of a work, I like to get an overview. I'd rather see the whole movie before I freeze a frame for inspection, or finish the novel before I analyse the opening of chapter 3. This overview is bound to be provisional: the details, when I go on to look at them more closely, may complicate the picture. But I need to find my way, tentatively at least, to a shape, or a project.

What preliminary purchase can we get on 'A slumber

did my spirit seal'? Briefly, it records that a once living being, who seemed as if she would never change, is dead and buried. Two separate states are contrasted, along with two moments: *then*, when she seemed immune to time; *now*, when she has lost all movement, all sensation. Two distinct tenses identify past and present states, and the blank space on the page between the two verses separates these moments from one another. Two pronouns distinguish the topics: in the first verse, 'I' occupies the main ground and 'she' features only as she seemed to *me*; 'she' alone appears in the second verse. 'I' didn't see her as mortal; now 'she' doesn't see anything at all. Instead, she revolves in the turning earth, alongside non-human elements of the planet.

As even this crude summary indicates, a contrast depends, paradoxically, on resemblances. It is easy to compare two chairs, or even a chair and a table, since they have properties in common; it's more difficult to contrast a smartphone and a stinging nettle, or a raven and a writing desk (where would you begin?). In 'A slumber', the terms of the comparison resemble each other but they change places. Then, in the past, 'I' was blind to the possibility of change, sealed off from awareness of time, oblivious; 'she' is oblivious now. 'I' lacked part of what it is to be human; now she lacks everything that distinguishes human beings from the objects of nature. 'She' seemed unchanging, and now she is beyond the reach of change. 'She', who seemed to escape the ordinary laws that govern the earth, has been incorporated into the earth itself.

'She' was a 'thing' – strange word, but not impossible. Shakespeare's Valentine calls his beloved Silvia 'a thing divine', while Miranda uses the same phrase as she falls in love with Ferdinand: 'I might call him / A thing divine, for nothing natural / I ever saw so noble'. In both these instances, the term points to an unearthliness that also defines the 'she' of 'A slumber', who seemed to 'my' sealed-off, fearless spirit, safe from mortality. But the supernatural 'thing' of the first verse has become, in the second, a thing in a more obvious sense, an object that joins other natural objects, listed as rocks and stones and trees.

'I'

This close parallel between one state and another, while preserving their difference, allows the poem to encompass a surprisingly complex story in a small space. But mysteries remain. We know nothing more about the 'I' of the poem; 'she' clearly matters, but why? She might be a lover, a mother, a sister, a child (or a pet dog, come to that). Critics, compelled by the poem's unassuming eloquence, tantalised by what it doesn't reveal, and wanting the tale it tells to be true, have sought to replace its pronouns with proper names. They prefer, in other words, to find something beyond the words on the page, to identify a point of reference outside the poem that will validate or substantiate it.

Common sense proposes that any statement is a message coming from an identifiable source. But is common sense always right, especially when it comes to what I have broadly called fiction? What does it mean to say 'I' in a text that presents itself as a lyric? Can we assume that on the other side of a piece of writing which appears in a book of poetry there subsists a person who is undergoing the emotions depicted, or that the story it tells must be factual? Do we need to put to the test of accuracy George Wither's claim that 'I loved a lass, a fair one'? When Cole Porter writes 'I've got you under my skin', does it have to be a statement of fact? Don't lyrics rather work by embracing anyone, all of us? The application of any number of standard love songs ('Cheek to cheek', 'The very thought of you', 'Blue moon') is so indefinite that they can be performed by a singer of either sex.

There is much to lose in the process of reducing a lyric to reality. Ben Jonson wrote about the fictional 'I' in one of his 'Elegies', 'Let me be what I am'. His argument, roughly paraphrased, is that the real-life poet might be decrepit, obese and cold-hearted but, for his love poems to work, his readers have to see him as young, agile and in love – not so much in reality as in the illusion the words create. There is room for a discrepancy, then, between the writer in the tavern and the person brought to life by the poem. Lyric poetry hovers in the margin between fact and fiction. An individual work may lean one way or the other and an issue for the critic is that we can never be sure quite where we stand. A great deal of energy has been expended on the story 'behind' Shakespeare's Sonnets, for example, apparently without reference to the fact that Shakespeare was a full-time dramatist, capable of entering with equal conviction into the states of mind of assassins, clowns, pickpockets, sons in mourning, drunkards, irate fathers, innocent virgins and young women married in secret. When sonneteers declare themselves in love, they might be – or they might just want to write a love sonnet to be proud of.

Is it part of a critic's job to decide how far a poem is autobiographical? And, if we could, what difference would it make to our understanding of the work? 'A slumber did my spirit seal' was written by William Wordsworth in the winter of 1798–9, when the author was in Germany with his sister Dorothy. It was published in 1800 in the second, expanded edition of *Lyrical Ballads*. Perhaps because they found the poem so believable, so genuine, an older generation of critics took for granted that 'I' was Wordsworth himself and chose to read the poem in the light of his other work. One train of thought led to the identification of a personal death wish on the part of the poet. Wordsworth loved nature; rocks and stones and trees were his anchors and moral guardians; 'she' was privileged to be among them; Wordsworth must envy her.

It's possible. But I personally find that reading difficult to reconcile with the blank negations of the poem: 'No motion', 'no force'; 'She neither hears nor sees'. And I cannot read the heavy monosyllables of the last line as celebrating her union with the natural objects listed. In other words, that interpretation seems to look somewhere beyond the poem, not *at* it. But what do *you* think?

There is, meanwhile, another, more textual way to invoke the author in the course of explaining the credibility of 'A slumber'. The edition of *Lyrical Ballads* where the poem first appeared was prefaced by a justification of this experimental volume. The project, Wordsworth declared, was to break with the kind of heroic, poeticising language readers were used to. An 'Advertisement' at the beginning of the first edition condemns the conventional poetry of the time for its 'gaudiness and inane phraseology'. In the second edition, where 'A slumber' appears, the prefatory vocabulary is toned down but the implication remains that eighteenth-century verse had allowed self-conscious stylistic elevation to take the place of genuine feeling.

William Wordsworth, 1770–1850. Prolific writer, Poet Laureate 1843–50. One of the first generation of Romantic poets, at first inspired by the French Revolution but later repelled by its brutality, he spent much of his life in the Lake District. *The Prelude*, his own account of the role of nature in his poetic formation, was first completed in 1806 but not published until it appeared, much revised, after his death.

By contrast with convention, the Preface to the second edition maintains, *Lyrical Ballads* will present 'a selection of the real language of men in a state of vivid sensation'. The material of the poems will be 'the primary laws of our nature' and 'the essential passions of the heart', depicted without restraint and in plain and simple terms. Accordingly, the manner of writing is to be natural, at least as far as is compatible with the pleasures allowed by metre and rhyme.

The intense feelings of ordinary people, in other words, defined in everyday language, will give the experience reality. We follow Wordsworth to the degree that we too associate a lack of affectation with authenticity. 'A slumber' gives the impression of transparency; its unassuming manner seems to guarantee its truth as an expression of personal emotion. The vocabulary is almost entirely Anglo-Saxon, with the exception of 'diurnal', a favourite of eighteenth-century poetic diction but justified here, perhaps, by the solemnity of its place in the poem. On only two occasions do the words depart from the patterns of ordinary speech. The first line adopts a 'poetic' word order, no doubt because 'A slumber sealed my spirit' wouldn't rhyme or scan. 'No motion has she' seems motivated by other considerations, since 'She has no motion' would have fitted the metre just as well. Here the inversion places special emphasis on the opening negative. Otherwise, the sentence structure is as familiar as the vocabulary. And the poem's brevity seems to confirm the sincerity of the utterance. What is there to say, after all, about the bleak fact of death?

In addition, 'A slumber' is a ballad. Its manner emulates the folk tradition, which has always laid claim to the direct, unassuming depiction of elemental passions. The title of *Lyrical Ballads* is not accidental. Augustan poets, heirs of Milton and Dryden, valued the high style and Latinate sentence structure, as well as classical vocabulary and allusions. But with the new interest in the Gothic Middle Ages, a populist counter-current began to emerge in the decades before the French Revolution. It is worth looking closely at the full title of Thomas Percy's influential anthology, published in 1765: *Reliques of Ancient English Poetry: Consisting of Old Heroic Ballads, Songs, and Other Pieces of our Earlier Poets, (Chiefly of the Lyric Kind)*. True to the compression that characterises the contents themselves, *Lyrical Ballads* effectively abridges Percy's own title.

RELIQUES

OF

ANCIENT ENGLISH POETRY:

CONSISTING OF

Old Heroic BALLADS, SONGS, and other
PIECES of our earlier POETS,

(Chiefly of the LYRIC kind.)

Together with some few of later Date.

VOLUME THE SECOND.

DURAT OPUS VATUM

LONDON:
Printed for J. DODSLEY in Pall-Mall.
M DCC LXV.

Thomas Percy joins the Gothic revival.

'A slumber' is spare, like the folk ballads; the work mimics their abrupt transitions; it echoes the commonest of the ballad rhythms, with four stressed syllables in the first line and three in the second. Here is the opening of 'The ballad of Sir Patrick Spens', included in Percy's collection:

The king sits in Dunferling town,
    Drinking the blood-red wine.

Compare:

A slumber did my spirit seal;
    I had no human fears.

'Drinking' reverses the stresses in the second line of 'Sir Patrick Spens', and we could argue about where to put the stress on 'sits in'. Wordsworth's poem simply tidies up the minor irregularities of the traditional work.

Like 'A slumber', the ballads tell a story, however short, and it's commonly a bleak one. They depict a life of hardship and violence: Sir Patrick is drowned at sea, along with his ship and all its crew. The 'she' of 'A slumber' is also lost, absorbed not by the sea but by the daily rotating earth. Both death and love are familiar topics among the traditional ballads. In 'The unquiet grave',

The wind doth blow today, my love,
    And a few small drops of rain;
I never had but one true-love,
    In cold grave she was lain.

The unnamed lover mourns for a year and a day, until the corpse speaks from the grave to ask why he will not let her rest. He begs for one last embrace, but the dead woman replies, 'If you have one kiss of my clay-cold lips, / Your time will not be long'. The narration is elliptical; nothing is explained or contextualised; the vocabulary is as everyday as the language of 'A slumber'. But this ballad puts itself before us as a ghost story: it lays no claim to truth. Like most ballads, 'The unquiet grave' is anonymous: no one in their right mind would try to identify the characters.

The Preface to *Lyrical Ballads*, along with other pronouncements by Romantic poets on their immediate predecessors, has proved so influential that modern readers are often agreeably surprised when they find the eighteenth-century poetry it condemns more pleasurable than they had been led to expect. We are heirs of Wordsworth to the degree that we take a simple manner as evidence of genuine feeling. But it's wise to be aware that the greatest art lies in concealing art. The plain style, in other words, may require more skill than any number of fancy comparisons. Possibly, we underestimate the skill of 'A slumber' if we succumb to its promise of the unadorned truth? Perhaps the poem, like so many of the other *Lyrical Ballads*, is closer to fiction than critics have supposed.

'SHE'

If 'I' was conventionally identified as Wordsworth himself, who was 'she'? This question has excited intense speculation among those critics who like to look outside the work in order to substantiate the genuineness of the feeling it depicts. At its first appearance in 1800, the untitled poem was placed immediately after two lyrics about a 'Lucy'. In the first, 'Strange fits of passion I have known', the 'I' of the poem is identified as a lover who, on the way to Lucy's cottage, is suddenly overcome by an unaccountable fear that she might be dead. In the second, 'Song' ('She dwelt among th' untrodden ways'), Lucy is an unknown maiden, now in her grave. It followed from its position immediately after these two poems, or so it was generally held, that the unnamed 'she' of 'A slumber' must be Lucy too.

Wordsworth's *Poems* of 1815 separated 'A slumber' from the first two, however. This time, the lyric was preceded by another work about a Lucy who died when she was three. But it was Victorian editors who put together the group that appears in my *Selected* Wordsworth. Here, five poems, numbered in sequence, appear under the single heading, *Lucy*, with 'A slumber' as the third. What was at first a provisional identification has now turned into an inescapable fact.

There were exceptions to this rule. Some critics, who might have been happier as grammarians, thought the real protagonist of 'A slumber' must be 'my spirit', since this was the only candidate named before the 'she' who appears so abruptly at the beginning of the third line. My spirit was so fast asleep that now it is virtually dead. This seems to me to stretch a point, not least because it ignores a long tradition of unidentified lyric shes who don't usually cause any anxiety. When William Congreve begins a poem of the same length as 'A slumber' with 'False though she be', we don't ask for a name, any more than we do with 'She loves, you, yeah, yeah, yeah', or 'She may be the face I can't forget'.

Let me offer you, as a digression, and purely for the pleasure of it, one of my favourite complete poems in this mode by Robert Herrick:

> Her pretty feet
> Like snails did creep
> A little out, and then,
> As if they started at Bo-peep,
> Did soon draw in again.

Herrick is so obviously playful that we don't worry about who owns the feet so coyly appearing and retreating under voluminous skirts. Does it necessarily follow from the elegiac character of Wordsworth's subject matter that we have to be correspondingly solemn about the identity of his unnamed female figure?

Meanwhile, 'Lucy' was giving rise to at least two problems. First, the succeeding poem in the 1800 volume, a fable about 'The waterfall and the eglantine' had nothing whatever to do with any Lucy. Proximity evidently does not guarantee continuity. And second, no one has been able to identify a Lucy who features in Wordsworth's life story. Instead, 'Lucy' was a conventional name for a doomed love in eighteenth-century verse, and a ballad about a Lucy who died of love featured in Percy's *Reliques*. For these reasons, even if 'she' was Lucy, and a young woman, the identification still did not gratify the desire to ground the poem in fact.

A comment on 'A slumber' by Samuel Taylor Coleridge, Wordsworth's close friend and collaborator in *Lyrical Ballads*, has prompted investigation of a wide range of real-life candidates for the role of Lucy. Coleridge copied out the poem in a letter to his friend Thomas Poole, calling it a 'sublime Epitaph'. 'Whether it had any reality, I cannot say', Coleridge noted. 'Most probably, in some gloomier moment he had fancied the moment in which his sister might die'. Was 'she' Dorothy Wordsworth, then? But Coleridge wasn't sure. So how about Annette Vallon, William's French lover? Or his wife, Mary Hutchinson? The problem here is that all these were alive and well in 1798–9, which pushed the poem back in the direction of fiction, the fantasy of 'some gloomier moment', and so still failed to supply it with a basis in reality. Was 'Lucy', perhaps, an unidentified childhood sweetheart, now dead? A further contender, Margaret Hutchinson, Mary's sister, had died in 1796 at the age of 24. Was Margaret both Lucy and the 'she' of the poem?

Samuel Taylor Coleridge, 1772–1834. Poet, critic and literary theorist. His most famous contribution to *Lyrical Ballads* was 'The Rime of the Ancient Mariner', a ballad, but in some ways unlike any other. His lectures on Shakespeare were highly influential, while his critical philosophy is summarised in *Biographia Literaria* (1817).

It's possible. There is no evidence whatever to support this view but, if we're not careful, conjecture hardens into truth: more than one critic is convinced that 'A slumber' is about Margaret Hutchinson; Wordsworth was evidently in love with her and her early death made him for the first time aware of mortality. And suddenly a lyric poem draws its meaning from the tradition of romantic novels. As a corrective, it might be worth remembering that Coleridge was saying that he didn't know who 'she' was, or even whether she had any real existence.

Just to show how easy it is to concoct these stories, let me make up another that conflicts with the preceding one but would work, I believe, just as well. Perhaps 'A slumber' is not about someone who died young. If it only seemed that she could not feel the touch of earthly years, shouldn't we construe that she did in fact age, without appearing to? Not a lover but, just as important, a mother, then? *Lyrical Ballads* also includes 'We are seven', a poem about a girl of eight years old who cannot recognise that her two dead siblings are irretrievably lost. Although she knows Jane and John are in the churchyard, even though their deaths reduce the children of the family to five, 'We are seven', she insists, and the Preface explains that the poem concerns the inability of childhood to come to terms with the notion of death. Can it be a coincidence that Wordsworth was eight when his mother died? Yes, it can, but critics who insist on grounding poems in fact would not settle for that. Drawing on another poem in the volume, it is possible to turn 'her' into Wordsworth's mother; the slumber that sealed his eight-year-old spirit was childhood innocence; now, as a grown-up, he knows what death means.

One admired critic, J. Hillis Miller, invoked psychoanalysis to have it both ways: Lucy is a fictional young woman who takes the place of Wordsworth's actual mother. Alone and bewildered, the poet himself wants to join them both, to be dead but without actually dying, a part of nature and at the same time aware of it in his capacity as a living being. There is a good deal more where that came from, but I'll give you the reference at the back of the book and leave you to pursue it if you want to.

On all these readings the real subject of the poem is 'I', the poet, Wordsworth, who is seen to acquire the knowledge of mortality. But he does so at the expense of the woman who is now consigned to the earth. Mastery goes to the poet, who has profited, however sorrowfully, from a woman's death, to discover a significant truth. Wordsworth has achieved wisdom. And more mastery goes to the critic, who has carried out research on the poet's life in order to pin down an elusive lyric. The critic has taken possession of the poem, has probed its secret and revealed what it has to teach us: that we deny change at our peril; people die; Wordsworth knows this because Lucy/Margaret/his mother died.

I'm not convinced. But what do *you* think?

AN ALTERNATIVE

In these cases the poem is seen as incomplete as it stands. The assumption is that the critic's job is to complete it by bringing in outside information, in the process elucidating its moral purpose. As you may detect, I am not entirely happy about this traditional approach to interpretation, which assumes that the task of the critic is to supply what is left out by the words themselves, locating their true theme in the mind of the author, in order to uncover an ethical truth. The procedure involves slightly too much moral instruction for my taste, a good deal too much conjecture, and altogether too much mastery. While the psychology is no more than speculative, the teaching is in the end banal. I recoil slightly from assuming the poem needs outside help, or believing we make it ours by solving its puzzles.

Suppose, then, for the sake of argument, that we try something different, treating 'A slumber' as a lyric rather than a diary entry. This would mean ignoring the conjectural identifications, allowing the pronouns to remain opaque, while leaving the poem to hover in the margin between fact and fiction. We'd assume that it was not in need of repair from outside and surrender our desire to uncover ethical designs on the reader. Instead, we'd see 'A slumber' as dramatising an encounter with an irreparable loss. In those circumstances, we might notice that the 'I' disappears after the first two lines. 'I' is not the subject of what follows: 'she' is. And she, who seemed impervious to death, is now absorbed by the earth: a unique and valued person (or possibly pet) is lost in the indifference of mortality. The bleak meaning of unheralded bereavement is now the poem's theme. There is no relief there, and no profit to be derived from the experience. If 'A slumber' records a victory of any kind, the triumph belongs to death, which reduces living human beings to the level of rocks and stones and trees.

This would give us a genuinely radical – experimental – elegy. In a long tradition of poetic laments for the dead it was conventional to acknowledge the tragedy of loss but also to offer consolation of one kind or another. Were the critics seeking moral instruction from Wordsworth's poem unconsciously asking it to meet expectations derived from this tradition? Among the elegies we can expect Wordsworth to have known, Milton's *Lycidas*, grand, classical, ornate, is as far removed as can be from the manner of 'A slumber'. But there too, whatever the individual John Milton might have felt about the loss of his fellow-poet Edward King in 1637, the narrator of the pastoral fiction is first desolate at the loss of a close companion who will never return. Demoralised by the perpetual threat of sudden death, the 'I' of this poem nevertheless recovers a sense of purpose: Lycidas lives on in heaven – and here, now, on earth there is work for a poet to do. Meanwhile, Shakespeare, a constant point of reference in Wordsworth's writing, builds a different kind of comfort into the most delicate of elegiac songs from *Cymbeline*: 'Fear no more the heat o' th' sun, / Nor the furious winter's rages.' And when William Collins, admired by the young Wordsworth, rewrites Shakespeare's dirge, he brings in living nature as the consoling setting of the grave:

> The red-breast oft at evening hours
>> Shall kindly lend his little aid:
> With hoary moss and gathered flowers,
>> To deck the ground where thou art laid.

Against this background, 'A slumber' stands out – aligns itself with the ballad tradition, perhaps – in its stark refusal to seek any compensation for the repeated negatives that define extinction.

IMPASSE

Could 'A slumber' be a fiction about anonymous protagonists and still stand as a moral fable? Less convincingly, I think. The acquisition of wisdom that critics have found in the poem is not mentioned there; it requires them to conjure the figure of an informed self who stands behind the words, exercising hindsight as their narrator or author. Only by naming the 'I' as Wordsworth or his surrogate can we credibly identify the hero as someone who has learnt from experience. Could we have a story of unredeemed desolation and keep Wordsworth as the 'I' in question? Conceivably, but the moralising that Wordsworth doesn't hesitate to practise elsewhere easily bleeds into a reading of this work too.

Two distinct readings, then, centring on either gain or loss. On one interpretation, the poem teaches a consciousness of what it is to be human; on the other, it names, as far as that's possible in words, the feeling of bereavement. True, the moral in the first reading includes an encounter with the bleakness of death, but in a good cause, a sharpened awareness understood as instructive. On this pious account of the poem, Wordsworth, and, by implication, the reader, are now sadder but wiser. On the alternative reading, the reader is invited to enter into a sadness for which no solace is available. One view leaves us confident and knowing, the other participating for the duration in the 'human fears' the protagonist once lacked.

Look at it one way, and it works. Look at it the other way, and it still works. Yet, since each reading excludes the other, it is impossible to look at it both ways at the same time. Self-evidently you, as an individual reader, are free to decide, to opt for either account, or to oscillate between them. As I have indicated, I prefer the second view. But *criticism* faces a larger question. As far as I can see, the two distinct readings depend on different understandings of what criticism *is* and what it's *for*. One looks for moral instruction, the other for passion. One looks beyond the work, the other at it. In these circumstances, there is no authority we can appeal to for a decision on which is right (or which is wrong, since 'right' might be unduly optimistic about what interpretation can achieve).

If two versions of criticism are in play here, two distinct accounts of language are also in operation. One seeks an anchor for meaning in the world, and comes up with iden-tities for those shifters, 'I' and 'she', in order to hold them in place. The other allows the possibility that our under-standing of the words 'I' and 'she' does not depend on refer-ence to specific persons. In other words, interpretation does not require a foothold for meaning outside language itself. Instead, it chooses to retain the mobility of the pronouns, and settles for a corresponding degree of uncertainty.

There will be more – much more – to say about how lan-guage works in due course. For the moment, can we agree that, whatever the preference of a particular critic, criti-cism faces an impasse? We can't show conclusively that 'I' is Wordsworth; we can't be certain of the opposite. In the last analysis, the project of 'A slumber' is undecidable.

If you concede this much, what follows? Does undecid-ability mean that anything goes, that readers can legitimately make what they like of the text, or that 'it's all subjective'? On the contrary. There are limits to the range of interpretations the words will bear. For example, I have suggested that 'A slumber' could be about a pet dog. That would make sense of 'thing', as well as 'no human fears' (I was just like the dog, unaware of mortality). Alternatively, the poem could be a confession of murder while of unsound mind: 'I' didn't share the normal human fear to kill, because I didn't believe she was mortal; now there she lies ... Admissions of murder are not uncommon in the ballad tradition. What's more, murder recurs as a theme of *Lyrical Ballads*: 'The thorn' concerns infanticide; the jealous lover of 'Ellen Irwin' kills her by accident.

There is not much support for either reading in the poem itself. The absence of references to trustful eyes and wet noses calls in question the assumption that the theme is a dog. Meanwhile, the belief that she wasn't subject to death from old age is not the same as assuming she could not be murdered. But however unlikely these readings of 'A slumber' might seem, we can't absolutely rule them out. Criticism necessarily involves judgements and not all of them are about the value of the work. Instead, some concern the plausibility of alternative interpretations. (William Empson once noted that good sense was a quality urgently required in critics.) Although the poem doesn't provide much evidence in support of either the canine or the homicidal reading, the words would just about allow one or the other. The same work could not, however, by any stretch of possible meanings that I can see, be about the State Opening of Parliament or a visit to Disneyland. Undecidability is an effect of words and their capacity for more than one interpretation, not a consequence of the power of a reader to jet off into a personal fantasy and leave the words behind. Readers must – and no doubt will – do what they like, but they cease to be critics when they disregard the words.

FORM

In the course of discussing 'A slumber', I have paid a good deal of attention to its formal properties, specifically vocabulary, tenses, word order, metre and structure. I have silently taken for granted a good deal of assonance, or resemblances between sounds ('rocks, stones'), as well as alliteration, or repeated consonants ('slumber', 'spirit', 'seal'), not to mention a combination of the two ('Rolled round'). In other works, metaphor might contribute more than it does here. Doesn't the bare literalness of the second verse of 'A slumber' play a part in the impression it creates of authenticity?

Because I don't want to risk reducing criticism to box-ticking, I have not isolated these topics but incorporated them into the discussion, as critics do. Even so, there is something to be said for paying conscious and deliberate attention to the formal properties of the work. Unless we look for them explicitly, they may well appear transparent, but in practice they play a major role in constructing and containing the range of possible responses. Good criticism is alert to form and acknowledges its role in the production of meaning.

PREVAILING CURRENTS

Is Wordsworth's poem a special case? Yes and no. Every work is a special case in one way or another. But 'A slumber' raises questions that to varying degrees confront critics of other works. If, to my regret, matters of form don't always attract the attention they deserve, three preoccupations dominate conventional criticism. While evaluation is widely taken for granted as the object of the exercise, many critics associate value with the delivery of moral instruction or ethical truths. And it is not unusual to seek the author 'behind' the work as the guarantee of its meaning.

We do not have to swim with the prevailing currents: every one of these preoccupations is open to a range of objections. But before we come to those, the next step will be to investigate how criticism came to lay so much stress on those three issues: value, morality and the author.

2

HOW DID WE GET HERE?

OTHER DAYS, OTHER WAYS

So prevalent in current criticism are evaluation, the quest for morality and speculation about the author that they might be taken for natural or inevitable. But it wasn't always so. Among the earliest Western critics, Plato denounced fiction in general as a thoroughly bad influence and much subsequent critical argument set out to reverse this view. In these cases evaluation was inseparable from morality; in other instances, assessments of worth relied on formal rules. But as time went by, criteria of judgement that had seemed obvious in one epoch were rejected by another. Invocation of the author's life as explanation of the work, meanwhile, was a late development and still provokes debate, not least when the private lives of admired artists fail to stand up to scrutiny.

All this deserves detailed discussion, but first, a curiosity. Although there is very little evidence of how ordinary people interpreted fiction in the past, one undervalued treasure remains to us – and it shows no interest whatever in either judgement or the author, while extracting a rather unexpected moral. Simon Forman, a London doctor, kept a record of his visits to the Globe Theatre in 1610–11. His accounts of the plays centre on the plots. He records the story of *Macbeth*, for example, just as if it had actually happened in front of him. Macbeth and Banquo were riding through a wood, when they encountered three women fairies or nymphs (he doesn't call them witches). As the events unfold, Forman is very struck by Banquo's ghost – and by a detail that might appear incidental to anyone but another physician. When Lady Macbeth sleepwalked, confessing her guilt, 'the doctor noted her words'.

There is nothing about whether Forman admired the play, although his enjoyment may be inferred from his close attention to the plot. Nor is there any concern with Shakespeare himself: in fact, the playwright doesn't get a mention. But Forman is evidently pleased to find his own similitude on the stage. In addition, although he also liked to profit morally from his playgoing, the great truths some of us expect from works we value are not quite what Forman looks for. His account of *The Winter's Tale* says nothing of Leontes' long repentance or, indeed, its reward in Hermione's resurrection, surely the most striking episode for modern audiences. On the other hand, he pays close attention to the subterfuges of the con-man Autolycus, who extracts money by pretending to have been robbed, and Forman's record ends with a memo to self: 'Beware of trusting feigned beggars or fawning fellows'.

Simon Forman, 1552–1611. After a patchy education and failing to complete his course at Oxford, Forman became a schoolteacher, then a doctor, as well as a prophet, finally prophesying his own death.

It might not be wise to think of Simon Forman as a typical early modern playgoer. We know that he dabbled in the occult, for example, that orthodox physicians accused him of quackery, and that he had strong sexual appetites. But what would it mean to be typical, then or now? Am I a typical reader? Are you? Surely not.

GREEKS DISAGREE

It's hard to know where typicality is to be found. In general, people who hold the beliefs that prevail in their own time may well remain silent: they have no cause to take a stand. In consequence, we have no way of knowing what they thought. Instead, a position more commonly emerges as a protest against a previous view, or against the prevailing orthodoxy itself. Unlike Simon Forman, Aristotle was not so much recording what he saw on the stage as engaging in a debate with his great predecessor, Plato. The issue between them was the value of fiction in general, rather than the principles promoted by individual works. Plato was at odds with customary convictions about whether fiction was good for society.

The humanities, as we might now call them, played a substantial part in Greek education. Homer, Hesiod and the dramatists were all on the syllabus, and not only introduced the young to their culture but also offered instruction in divinity and ethics. Plato deplored this practice. As far as he was concerned, fiction was largely lies. Was this on the reasonable grounds that the revered Greek epics told of one-eyed giants and enchantresses who turned men into animals, as well as death-squads concealed in wooden horses? Not entirely: the problem went deeper. In the first instance, writers and artists had no access to truth itself, because all that even realists could do was imitate what they saw in this world. According to Plato's model of the cosmos, what we perceive around us is no more than a copy of the Forms, the perfect Ideas of things as they exist in the mind of God – true good, true beauty and so on. Fiction, representing (re-presenting) what we perceive, subsists at two removes from reality, offering mere shadows of shadows.

It followed from this that art was socially useless. In Plato's world, craft is valued because it serves a purpose: the work of architects, carpenters, shoemakers may be imperfect, no more than an aspiration to the Ideal building, bed or pair of shoes, but it satisfies a human requirement. Artists, by contrast, copy the copies, merely depicting or delineating palaces, couches and footwear. Without the skill to create such objects for use, artists offer nothing worth having.

Moreover, their products might do positive harm. Poetry, Plato points out, reproduced myths showing the deities on Mount Olympus as quarrelsome, venal and vindictive. In Plato's view, this grossly misrepresented God, who was perfection itself and could never do wrong. What was more, in the stories these culpable immortals interfered in the affairs of human beings and were to blame for many of their troubles. The image of human misery as divinely ordained or fated, Plato thought, discouraged the development of a sense of personal responsibility.

At the time, Greek schoolboys were expected to recite

the work of the canonical writers, and to do so with feeling, entering into the spirit of the passages they rehearsed and the characters portrayed there. It could not be good practice, Plato argued, to encourage the habit of speaking from the perspective of the wicked, the unjust or the despairing, when the object of education must be to instil virtue and self-control. Identity was a fragile thing, easily led astray, and fiction put poor models of human behaviour before those least equipped to resist it. On the basis of their immoral content, Plato recommended the excision of selected passages of the *Odyssey* and the *Iliad*, though his targets were not those references to sex and violence that we might now expect. Instead, what most bothered him was the depiction of the underworld as a place of sorrow, where spirits have lost their individuality and flit mindlessly to and fro in the gloom. How, he asked, could such images foster courage in the face of death?

In other words, Plato makes value judgements, but not on the quality of the writing. He has little to say about how individual works compare, and he shows no interest in the life of the author. Since in his view the arts endanger the making of good citizens and an ideal commonwealth, he ends by banishing fiction from his utopian Republic.

Plato, c. 428–347 BCE. Shocked by the execution of Socrates, Plato left Athens for some years, eventually returning to establish his Academy just outside the city. His dialogues debate issues of ethics and politics, and their topics range from the structure of the physical world to the nature of love.

FOOTNOTES TO PLATO

Plato's influence on Western culture is unsurpassed. In the light of his pronouncements, particularly on the worthlessness of fiction and its immoral influence, writers and critics have repeatedly found themselves on the defensive.

Among those who have felt called on to vindicate their work, Philip Sidney and Percy Bysshe Shelley, in their respective *Defences* of poetry, chose to occupy some of the moral ground staked out by Plato, while reversing his value judgements.

Sir Philip Sidney, 1554–86. Author of the prose romance *Arcadia* as well as *Astrophil and Stella*, a sonnet sequence that influenced Shakespeare's Sonnets. *The Defence of Poesy*, also published as *An Apology for Poetry*, appeared in 1595, after his death from wounds received in battle in the Netherlands.

Percy Bysshe Shelley, 1792–1822. Radical and visionary, he wrote much lyric verse, including *Adonais*, an elegy for John Keats; a tragedy, *The Cenci*; and a lyric drama, *Prometheus Unbound*. *A Defence of Poetry*, written in 1821, was not published until 1840.

Sidney countered Platonism with a version of itself, maintaining that poetic invention rises above the dull reality we know to touch the Ideal itself. Only fiction can depict a golden world, or portray models of heroism and virtue. Shelley, still more rhapsodic, saw poets as guardians of the highest principles, 'the unacknowledged legislators of the world'. Eventually, Matthew Arnold would propose that literature should fill the space vacated by religion, thus reverting, coincidentally or not, to a version of the conventional Greek model Plato was contesting in the first place. As a school inspector, Arnold was very anxious to include recitation by heart in the curriculum, prescribing exactly the practice Plato deplored. 'If a child is brought up', Arnold wrote in an 1882 report, 'as he easily can be brought, to *throw himself into* a piece of poetry, an exercise of creative activity has been set up in him quite different from the effort of learning a list of words to spell.'

Matthew Arnold, 1822–88. Poet, critic and commentator. Perhaps best known for *Culture and Anarchy* (1869), he continues to influence critical and educational attitudes today.

ARISTOTLE'S COUNTER-ARGUMENT

But all that was to come. The first Western thinker we know of to reinstate the moral value of what he called poetry was Aristotle, who had himself spent twenty years at Plato's Academy. Perhaps he saw an opening in *The Republic* itself, where Plato acknowledges the pleasure given by drama and poetry, especially the Homeric epics. If fiction could prove that it has a place in a well-run society, he would welcome it back in, Plato concedes. Aristotle argues that it merits such a place for pretty much the same reason as Plato wanted to expel it.

Towards the end of Plato's discussion of art, it emerges that fiction, and drama in particular, threaten not only schoolchildren but also the adult public. We are all of us subject to emotion but, in Plato's view, civilisation aspires to the rationality that comes from self-discipline. Fiction, by contrast, centres on the irrational, dwelling on psychological instability and foregrounding fierce pain, extremes of grief or anger. What survives of Greek tragedy would bear him out. Defiance of the state, family feuds, incest, the murder of husbands and children drive the plots, but what makes these plays so remarkable is their faithful depiction of the feelings that belong to such experiences. Short, focused, intense, Greek drama can still keep playgoers on the edge of their seats, as modern productions attest. In Plato's view, because

fiction represents the unreasonable, it also legitimates the loss of self-control, encouraging citizens to believe that indulgence in passion is natural and acceptable. (Some of the same issues arise in discussions of the depiction of sex and violence today. Does the

Kristin Scott Thomas as Sophocles's Electra, 2015

fictional representation of rape or torture make them look normal?)

Aristotle shares Plato's analysis but rejects the conclusion: in his view, the dramatisation of intensity is good. Tragedy's role, he argues, is precisely to generate pity and fear in the audience. It concerns some deed of horror, and the special gift of the writer – or is it, perhaps, a touch of madness? – is the ability to replicate the passions, arousing in the process corresponding emotions in the audience. By this means tragedy accomplishes the catharsis of such feelings.

Aristotle, 384–322 BCE. After acting as tutor to Alexander the Great, Aristotle returned to Athens, where he set up his own philosophical school, the Lyceum. He wrote on logic, ethics, physics and metaphysics, as well as rhetoric and poetics.

Debate has never entirely subsided on the meaning of *catharsis*. Aristotle's *Poetics* is not a completed and polished treatise. On the contrary, it reads more like lecture notes, sometimes doubling back on itself, promising a complete overview of the existing genres but stopping short, in the event, at epic and tragedy. The reference to catharsis reads like a throwaway – as if everyone knew what it was and took for granted that this was the effect of tragedy, or as if Aristotle himself had already defined it, as perhaps he had in a lost section of the text. The term is translatable as 'purging' or 'purification', and the physical analogy is presumably relevant. As far as we can tell, Aristotle is claiming that tragedy excites emotion with a view to releasing it safely in an appropriate setting.

Emerging from religious ritual, the performance of Greek drama was public and socially endorsed. Plays were presented at annual festivals, when dramatists competed for prizes awarded by a panel of judges. Successive performances went on all day in open-air amphitheatres that seated thousands of spectators. Does Aristotle, then, reproduce a shared view that the passions aroused were at the same time discharged or pacified, individually and collectively, for the benefit of society?

CHANGING RULES

Plato and Aristotle took diametrically opposite lines on the value of fiction in general. Evidently, however, the Greek judges were assessing individual plays. Since then, the ranking of specific works has become the critical norm and formal rules have been adopted as criteria of judgement. If the physical space between players and audience, or between the page and the reader, keeps fiction in a controlled environment, it is also made safe by the conventions of composition. Distinct genres follow different patterns, and the more evident the formula, the greater the sense of security. Social comedy implicitly promises to obey the rules and may even invoke them explicitly, as Miss Prism does in *The Importance of Being Earnest*: the good end happily, and the bad unhappily; 'that is what fiction means'. Predictability proves reassuring when romance regularly leads to marriage, detective stories can be relied on to bring the murderer to book, and the gunman leaves town as soon as the community is clean again.

Once the rules become prescriptive, on the other hand, they can blind critics to the distinctive character of a work that defies or ignores them. Formal regularities are dear to Aristotle, whose *Poetics* lays down the habits proper to tragedy and epic. But the desire to evaluate can easily ambush analysis; what in Aristotle was descriptive would in due course cement itself as a criterion of judgement. Subsequent critics were to take Aristotle's observations to heart and, some would say, to excess. In one instance, he notes among the differences between epic and drama that a play generally confines its unified action to a period of 24 hours. For the French classical theatre, this was to become a requirement for three 'unities'. To be worthy of the name, a tragedy, it was now believed, must represent a single event taking place in a single day and confined to a single location. By this measure, Shakespeare was judged wild and untutored.

Criteria of value, in other words, are subject to change. Aristotle also notes that the audience may have the greatest investment in a protagonist who is neither a saint nor a villain but an ordinary person who makes an error. We are still struggling to throw off what became an obligation to track down the error that vindicates the punishing outcome, the 'tragic flaw' that brings the death of the central figure into line with poetic justice. I was brought up to believe that the Duchess of Malfi, murdered on the instructions of her unhinged brother, must have deserved her fate because, as a young widow, she opted to remarry. Books are still emerging from the press to explain the weakness in Hamlet's character, quite ignoring the ambiguity of his predicament as a good man urged by a ghost of doubtful origins to repeat the crime of regicide alleged against his uncle.

Tragedy does not always exemplify fair play. As standards to judge by, then, the rules are unreliable. In practice, the reassuring regularities change from one culture to another, while different modes allow the prevailing conventions more or less visibility. In our own time, meanwhile, modernism has taught us that challenges to propriety can be exciting and may become imperative as predictability begins to stifle invention. On the other hand, no genre is rule-free. Even Antonin Artaud's convention-flouting Theatre of Cruelty, while it was happy to involve playgoers and, indeed, to assault their senses, was not so anarchic as to subject audience members to actual violence.

Awareness of the prevailing rules can help critics see what's going on; insistence on them can obscure it. The desire to judge all too easily leads on to the establishment of rigid criteria. Already in Aristotle's day criticism was a well-established practice and the philosopher sees it as his job to assess and soften its rigour. Critics find fault, he tells us, on the basis of five concerns: impossibility, improbability, corruption, contradiction and technical incorrectness. Most of these are offences against realism and Aristotle is fairly relaxed about the representation of what is unlikely or just plain inaccurate. Corruption is not to be tolerated but the depiction of depravity is not ruled out. Instead, it is allowed if it serves the interests of the plot as a whole.

Already, it seems, morality is not the only standard of judgement. Strict notions of what fiction ought to be are brought to bear on what it is. Aristotle is not averse to defining what the *best* tragedies do and he is stout in his defence of Homer, but he also indicates that an insistence on prior criteria can damage critical understanding. Meanwhile, there is no indication of any interest in individual authors, except in so far as their names are invoked to demarcate a body of work.

Among those who went on to codify more conventions and so lay down new standards for evaluation, some of the most influential have been practitioners themselves. The Roman poet Horace has carried a great deal of weight and critics writing today might be surprised to discover how far they are his descendants. Many people who have never consciously read a word of Horace's *Art of Poetry* know that the storyteller is well advised to begin *in medias res*, in the middle of things, or to avoid resolving the plot by means of a *deus ex machina*, a supernatural intervention from outside the tale. Horace affirmed the now widespread belief that fiction ought to teach and delight, or instruct by giving pleasure. He shared the Aristotelian view that what he calls poetry ought to affect the listener, creating a corresponding emotion in the audience. Much of his advice to the would-be author is plain sense in any epoch: don't take on what you can't do; avoid bombast; edit your work.

At the same time, his standards of evaluation also show how times change. Some of his observations throw into relief the cultural relativity of value judgements. Latin poetry allotted distinct metres to different poetic genres, and Horace is very preoccupied by the obligation to observe such discipline. None of this has much to say to modern poets. While he urges the dramatist to draw from life, in practice this turns out to mean reproducing conventional types: children should be changeable; young men idealistic but irresponsible; old men ought to enthuse over the past and complain about the young. While this representative behaviour is easy to recognise today, and might work well in farce, our commitment to individualism probably leads us to expect writers in other genres to complicate their characters. Indeed, we might well judge our authors by their ability to go beyond such stereotypes. What is praiseworthy in one epoch elicits blame in another.

Horace, 65 BCE–8 CE. Roman author of odes, satires and epistles concerned with how to live well. He enjoyed the patronage of the emperor Augustus. *The Art of Poetry* dates from about 17 BCE.

Criteria of judgement, then, are more than just personal but less than absolute. Assumptions about what fiction ought to be are as culturally variable as the rules themselves: both belong to convention. Alexander Pope's *Essay on Criticism*, sharp, witty, opinionated and shrewd, owes much to Horace but differs by offering advice explicitly to the critic, rather than the author. Criticism, Pope indicates, is now a way of life; 'witlings' everywhere are only too ready to give their views. What, then, should they look for in the work they set out to judge? Pope, who pays tribute to Aristotle, is equally ambivalent towards the rules, so ambivalent, indeed, that we might easily miss the characteristic sting in the tail of his couplet contrasting French and British practice. The servile French, he maintains, subject at this time to an absolute and autocratic monarchy, obey what they believe to be Aristotle's unities, while 'brave Britons', fierce defenders of liberty, remain unconquered – 'and uncivilised'.

In Pope's account, the real standard of judgement is nature; the conventions are no more than 'nature methodised'. This takes some unpicking. If flouting the rules is uncivilised, how can nature be the ideal? Pope thought of *nature* as the creative force in the universe. The natural order works well to produce beauty, harmony and balance, and creative writing will work equally well if it emulates nature, respecting the order centuries of writing have established as successful. Even so, rules are made to be broken by accomplished writers, and critics who cavil at every infraction of convention may well miss the point of the whole.

Alexander Pope, 1688–1744, poet, satirist and critic, best known for *The Rape of the Lock* (1712), the philosophical *Essay on Man* (1733–4) and *The Dunciad* (1728, 1742), a merciless exposé of the literary culture of the time.

So compelling are Pope's perfectly formed couplets, so convincing his practice of the values he preaches, that it would be easy to miss the gap between his notion of the fictional project and ours. Where the eighteenth century rates order and balance, we look for challenge and surprise. Twenty-first-century writers probably do not share Pope's aspiration to 'What oft was thought, but ne'er so well expressed'. Something, of course, depends on how we read this aphorism. Does it point to an idea that fiction formulates deeply felt but inarticulate experiences? The context in the poem would suggest not. Is Pope, conversely, asking fiction to set out the prevailing commonplaces with a stylistic flourish? Not quite that, either, I think, but something like the shared convictions of human *nature*, named, formulated, made perceptible in such an organised way as, paradoxically, to seem inevitable, *natural*.

OUR CRITERIA

And there lies the gap between Pope's world and our own, where individuality, cultural difference and the diversity of values so impress themselves on our consciousness that what remains of a shared human nature is reducible to a handful of banalities. The fiction we tend to rate highly more commonly brings differences into collision without any necessary obligation to reconcile them under an overarching harmony.

And in putting forward that idea, am I merely making up a new rule that critics can use to bludgeon works of our own time if they fail to conform? I hope not, but it's a risk. Rules are extremely seductive, and especially to critics, because they allow us to rationalise our preferences. And they are only the more persuasive when they remain undeclared, so apparently obvious that they need not be called rules at all. One assumption that comes into this category is the belief that fiction should be exactly like life. 'I wasn't convinced'; 'I didn't buy it.' How often is such a criterion invoked by even the most professional critics in order to condemn a work?

I myself am baffled by this insistence on two counts. First, if we want life, there is plenty of it about. Why demand it in fiction too? Second, the history of fiction reveals any number of possible modes besides realism: myth, allegory, romance, fantasy, satire … and these other modes may include much that is worth reading or pleasurable, without any obligation to replicate life. Should we dismiss the *Odyssey*, Aesop's *Fables*, *The Pilgrim's Progress*, *Tristram Shandy*, *Gulliver's Travels*, 'The Ancient Mariner' and *Frankenstein*, not to mention *Paradise Lost* and *Waiting for Godot*, because they don't replicate everyday existence? There are irresistible works of realism, no doubt of it, including *War and Peace* and *Middlemarch*. Moreover, they may be easier to get to grips with in the first instance. Soap opera and mass-market formula fiction also set out to create the illusion that plausible events are taking place before our very eyes. But easy is not the same as worth our attention, and we do ourselves an injustice when we invoke a rule to vindicate a preference for ready accessibility.

Preferences change. But I doubt whether recognising the relativity of value judgements will eliminate them. After all, we implicitly evaluate every time we choose one book rather than another, or recommend a film to a friend. Awareness that our assessments are provisional might encourage restraint, however. We may screen out other options if we let our judgement be bound by rules, spoken or unspoken.

Acknowledgement that no critical judgement is absolute or universal might also discourage the institutionalisation of evaluation as the primary purpose of English departments. That process, as I shall suggest in chapter 3, has had the unfortunate effect of dividing the field of culture.

DONNE'S WIFE

Moral assessment differs, formal criteria change, but none of the classic criticism I have mentioned shows any interest in the life of the author. Only Pope might seem to approach the question when he notes: 'A perfect judge will read each work of wit / With the same spirit that its author writ'. But this is not a move towards literary biography so much as a recommendation that the reader should look for the project of the work. We are best equipped to judge, Pope indicates, if we perceive the overall design, not a personal intention on the part of the writer.

In another part of the forest, however, something had begun to stir. After John Donne's death in 1631, Sir Henry Wotton undertook to write a life of his friend, the poet and Dean of St Paul's. But Wotton was a busy man and eight years later, when a collection of Donne's sermons was ready for the press, he himself died without having begun the task. Izaak Walton was pressed into service and in six weeks he produced a lively, readable, biographical preface to the book.

Biography was mainly the due of statesmen in the ancient world, and in the Middle Ages saints' lives represented an ideal of virtue and devotion. But occasionally a writer was thought worthy of a similar tribute. Fragments survive of the accounts of Horace, Terence and Lucan originally included by Suetonius in his record *Of Illustrious Men*, while it is thought that his life of Virgil was preserved as the work of the fourth-century Roman grammarian Aelius Donatus. When an English translation of the *Aeneid* was published in 1573, the work ascribed to Donatus was included in the prefatory material. Whoever composed it, 'The Life of Virgil' has classical authority. It records details of the poet's background, his precocious childhood and the exceptional qualities that brought him to the attention of the emperor Augustus. It also comments on the poems. But it makes no attempt to establish an explanatory relationship between the biography and the work.

Suetonius, 69 CE–after 122 CE. Roman biographer, author of *The Twelve Caesars*.

The life, we are invited to believe, is worth knowing about because of the virtues of the writing, but neither life nor writing is seen as a means to interpret the other. Giovanni Boccaccio's brief *Life of Dante* (literally *Pamphlet in Praise of Dante*) imitated the classical norm with variants. The work is a tribute to the poet but at the same time a reproach to Florence for driving such a great writer into exile, as well as a defence of vernacular poetry. Boccaccio records the facts of Dante's life and personality; he lists and praises his writings; once again, however, there is no interest in integrating the two, or accounting for the one in terms of the other.

Giovanni Boccaccio, 1313–75. Tuscan poet and scholar, best known for *The Decameron* and, from an English perspective, as a source for Chaucer and Shakespeare. *The Life of Dante* belongs to the 1350s.

In most respects, Walton's 'Life of Dr John Donne' followed the standard model, but it differed from the established pattern in a small but significant particular. One poem was traced to a specific event in the history of Donne's marriage. In 1611 Sir Robert Drury invited Donne to accompany him on an embassy to the French court. According to Walton, Anne Donne, expecting a baby at the time, regarded the prospect of her husband's absence with a nameless anxiety but, in view of their debt to Sir Robert's kindness, she reluctantly agreed that he should go. Two weeks later, Donne saw a phantom Anne walk twice through the room in Paris; her hair hung loose and she held a dead child in her arms. The messenger dispatched at once to London returned with the news that the child had been stillborn, leaving Anne ill in bed. It was as he left for Paris that Donne had given his wife 'A Valediction Forbidding Mourning' – and Walton transcribes a version of this poem apparently designed to console her.

Modern opinion is that the link between the poem and the occasion is purely conjectural. Lyrics about lovers parting were conventional, even if Donne's exceeds its genre: in practice, most of his *Songs and Sonnets* break with tradition in one way or another. Moreover, Walton himself admits that he was told the story by a third party and cannot confirm its accuracy. No part of the tale came from Donne himself. But Walton perfectly demonstrates the temptation few literary biographers are able to resist: a vivid anecdote, true or false, in conjunction with a personal origin for a piece of writing.

Izaak Walton, 1593–1683. Shopkeeper, fisherman and author of *The Compleat Angler*. Walton also wrote biographies of Henry Wotton, Richard Hooker, George Herbert and Robert Sanderson.

The problem, I find, is that the connection, once made, is hard to forget. Donne's elusive poem begins by comparing absence with death; only later does it seem to promise a homecoming. Between my reading and 'A Valediction', however, there now hovers the image of a pregnant wife, in distress because her husband's journey fills her with a strange fear that will in the event prove all too prophetic. The result is not only to dispel the elusiveness by reducing the poem to its supposed occasion but also to replace a tantalising lyric with a good story. Like many of the best biographies, Walton's life of Donne unintentionally competes with the text it is designed to explain. Another, simpler artefact supplants the work we're reading, solves its puzzles but, in the process, diminishes the strangeness that made it compelling.

LEONARDO'S MOTHER

A striking parallel was to occur in the field of visual art, when Sigmund Freud found a way to explain the enigmatic smile on the face of Leonardo da Vinci's *Mona Lisa*. Although Walton's life of Donne did not immediately prompt a spate of 'mind and work' accounts, the Romantic movement of the early nineteenth century would greatly encourage this new genre. Romanticism took for granted that the origins of the work could be found in the life of the writer. It was not the author but his widow who cemented the poem as autobiography when she supplied the title and subtitle of Wordsworth's *The Prelude, or, Growth of a Poet's Mind*. Even so, both have survived. Where in the seventeenth century Milton made poetry out of the fall of all human beings from a state of grace, Wordsworth's material was his personal fall from oneness with nature. If *The Prelude* claims to be the record of the moments that made him a poet, no wonder criticism sought an equally biographical explanation of 'A slumber did my spirit seal'.

A century later in 1910, when Freud published his life of Leonardo, it was widely assumed that biography would and should illuminate the products of creativity. But the psycho-analytic focus on the unconscious meant that the work was no longer explicable on the basis of deliberate intention or awareness. Instead, a reading might be expected to reveal more than the artist set out to say. No mean critic himself, Freud captures the ambiguity of the *Mona Lisa*'s expression, intelligible as tender or cruel from one moment to the next, and he quotes Walter Pater on the strange conjunction of all that is at once desirable and sinister in her 'unfathomable smile'. Alternatively seductive, magical or demonic, the smile singles out this portrait from others of its period, Freud agrees. But a similar smile reappears among Leonardo's other paintings, where a version of it, more serene, less dangerous, is also evident on the faces of the Virgin, Saint Anne and John the Baptist. The self-imposed task of the psychoanalyst is to explain how this obsessive smile came about.

Among his sources, Freud acknowledges Giorgio Vasari's sixteenth-century *Life of Leonardo*. True to its period, Vasari's biography provides some information about the artist's life and confers high praise on the works, but makes no attempt to account for the one in terms of the other. Vasari sees the smile as 'so pleasing that it was a thing more divine than human to behold'. Freud, however, finds its origin in the expression Leonardo's mother conjecturally turned on her son. Born out of wedlock, Leonardo was taken from his peasant mother, at or by the age of five, into the household of his father, the lawyer Ser Piero da Vinci. Freud's story – and he acknowledges help in composing it from the novelist Merezhkovsky – involves an unknown but devoted single mother, who poured out her love on the child and, in the process, robbed the fatherless boy of the opportunity to overcome the desire for his mother in a resolution of the Oedipus complex that would set him on the path towards heterosexuality. Her smile, in other words, while it promised unbounded affection, also threatened sexual privation in a world that condemned homoerotic acts. According to Freud, Leonardo was to re-find the same smile, lost object

Mona Lisa's unfathomable smile.

of desire and terror, in the sitter for the *Mona Lisa*, the wife of a wealthy Florentine silk merchant whose own history is as obscure as that of the artist's mother.

If Freud was an attentive critic, he was also a master

storyteller – and a great admirer of Sherlock Holmes. The biography of Leonardo unfolds with all the suspense of the best detective stories. Freud freely admits that much of his account is speculative. So closely integrated is the reading of the paintings with their supposed origin that it is no longer clear whether the life explains the work, or the work generates the biography. Freud begins from a feature of the painting but, in order to account for the smile, he invokes an inner life that cannot, by definition, be confirmed by the documents. It all fits perfectly together, so perfectly, perhaps, that once again one work of art confronts – and risks replacing – another. Leonardo's shadowy mother comes to life in the portrait of an equally mysterious woman, and offers to resolve the enigma of the painting. Doesn't all this, in consequence, also explain *away* the mystery that compels our attention?

Sigmund Freud, 1856–1939. Inventor of psychoanalysis. After training as a doctor, he studied in Paris with Jean-Martin Charcot, a neurologist interested in hypnosis and hysteria. Freud's recognition that the unconscious mind interacts with the body has influenced work in any number of intellectual fields.

'FACT' AND FICTION

Freud's life of Leonardo is probably the most colourful of all psychobiographies, but fiction was not slow to attract the attention of the new science. Ernest Jones, Freud's disciple, would locate the source of Hamlet's Oedipal reluctance to kill Claudius in the death of Shakespeare's father and the playwright's own rivalry in love. In evidence, he adduced the Sonnets, read as a transcription of fact.

Unlike Freud, Jones had nothing to say about his subject's early years, but our own epoch has let loose any number of psychobabblers ready to find the childhood of the writer wherever they look. One favourite is Dickens and the blacking factory. When he was twelve and his father was in the Marshalsea Debtors' Prison, the young Charles Dickens worked for some months labelling bottles of boot polish in order to contribute to the family income. This lowly employment interrupted the boy's education and he hated it. The episode has been cited again and again to explain the preoccupations of the novels with class, injustice, social aspiration and, of course, the Marshalsea itself.

And that is the problem with biographical criticism. The facts of a life can be seen as the origins of everything – and nothing. To my mind, a childhood spell of unpalatable employment does very little to illuminate the qualities that make the work of Dickens unique; it does not account for the phantasmic Miss Havisham, the outsize Mr Pickwick, or the menacing Mr Tulkinghorn. Nor can it explain a linguistic energy that makes the writing tumble over itself in its exuberance. At best, the blacking factory may have added impetus to the commentary on Victorian society that is so evident in the novels themselves. At worst, it offers an easy way to evade the critical challenge of locating the writing where it belongs in a line of descent from Shakespeare, Fielding, the Gothic and fairy tale. These elements reassemble and reconstitute themselves in Dickens's imagination to invent a world peopled by improbable comic, grotesque and threatening figures, all made to live in words as they could never do in reality.

Much author-biography is little more than high-level gossip and it can be just as compelling as gossip often is. In my view, however, it not only distracts attention from the work but also risks taking its place. Authors have experiences, and it may well be that these feed into their writing. So much goes without saying. Tying the work to the experience is a much more uncertain business, and there is a good deal to lose on the way. But don't take my word for it: many writers have protested against the reduction of their work to their life stories. Here, for example, is the Czech author Milan Kundera on the issue:

> The novelist demolishes the house of his life and uses its bricks to construct another house: that of his novel. From which it follows that a novelist's biographers unmake what the novelist made, and remake what he unmade. Their labor, from the standpoint of art utterly negative, can illuminate neither the value nor the meaning of a novel.

What we look for as critics has a major influence on what we find. If we seek the author 'behind' the writing, we shall uncover something, certainly, but it won't be the writing itself. If, conversely, we want to understand the work, that is surely where we need to look: at the writing, not elsewhere.

THE GLIMPSE OF AN ALTERNATIVE

Whatever convention dictates, there is always another option. Let's revisit the beginnings of Western criticism. Bracketing for the moment concern with the moral dangers or the benefits they claim, respectively, to identify, in my view both Plato and Aristotle were onto something important about the nature of fiction. Both agree that it represents or replicates powerful passions. The subject matter of fiction includes desire, fear, grief, revenge, all of them feelings we normally think of as private, intimate and visceral. Everyday exchange makes them hard to talk about, even to ourselves; no ordinary vocabulary seems to do them justice. That fiction puts on display cruelty and hatred, as well as love, doesn't imply approval of these conditions, any more than Shakespeare endorses the blinding of Gloucester or the murder of Desdemona. Whether inhumanity is normalised in the process depends on how it is depicted.

While representation may or may not include moral judgement, then, fiction's special character is that it brings to light or makes visible states of mind we may acknowledge but find it difficult to characterise in words. As in 'A slumber did my spirit seal', fiction aspires to do justice to situations where language commonly reaches its limits. In this respect, it addresses parts other practices cannot reach. Only the much later development of psychoanalysis comes close, and there the technical vocabulary commonly ensures that the writing keeps its distance, or names without actually setting out to convey the feeling itself.

Fiction alone actively brings its resources to bear on the

transmission of intensity, but it does so *as fiction*. That is to say it always presents itself as representation, as the product of imagination, not simple fact, and in the process fences off the emotion itself, averting a direct encounter with what might prove unbearable. While they may find themselves taut with suspense or in tears at the loss represented, playgoers do not, on the whole, invade the stage and put a stop to the atrocities taking place there; reading novels does not usually bring on post-traumatic stress disorder. However lifelike the illusion, it remains self-evidently illusory.

PLEASURE

Like Plato, Aristotle also made room for pleasure, and this was not merely the mask for an unpalatable moral. More mysteriously, the formality of fiction permits even what is most horrifying to be experienced as enjoyable. Aristotle includes the shape of the plot and language made delightful in his definition of tragedy. The rhythm of verse, the inventiveness of metaphor, wit, the practice of structural economy all offer to deepen the intensity and, paradoxically, generate pleasure at the same time. Without detracting from the pity of it, form can transfigure suffering.

Was Friedrich Nietzsche saying something of the kind, if more extravagantly, in *The Birth of Tragedy*? There he proposes that in Greek drama the force belonging to Dionysian instinctual life interacts with the dreamlike elevation of Apollonian art to create works that alleviate despair. Form, he claims, offers enchantment, rendering the playgoer's revulsion from pain and absurdity compatible with life; the tragedy that names suffering also tames it. There is much that is puzzling in this youthful book, and a good deal to disagree with; indeed, Nietzsche himself would later repudiate some of it. But he does offer an alternative to moralistic explanations of the curious fact that the depiction of grief gives pleasure.

Friedrich Nietzsche, 1844–1900. Professor of classical philology at Basel University from the age of 24. His work, always impatient with orthodoxy, remains controversial, not least thanks to its (mis)appropriation by National Socialism. It is now possible to recognise, however, that Nietzsche delivers a series of radical challenges to orthodox Western philosophy. *The Birth of Tragedy* was published in 1872.

Nietzsche may also have influenced Jacques Lacan, who would go on to build a theory of culture on the idea that art forms a magic circle round an emptiness that marks the place of the lost, archaic object of the drive. But that is an issue I have discussed elsewhere. Here, I suggest that we trace the role of criticism in shaping the assumptions of the young, as it entered into the school and university curriculum.

3

THE MAKING OF A DISCIPLINE

SCHOOL STORIES

As English teaching entered the school curriculum, it came to confirm, whether by accident or design, the three priorities of conventional criticism: value judgements were foundational, the best works delivered moral improvement, and their source and explanation was the mind of the author. But at the same time, the emergence of the discipline gradually encouraged the growth of other – and perhaps more fruitful – ways of perceiving the role of the critic.

English has not always been a classroom subject and criticism is a relative newcomer in the history of education. The story takes us back to the sixteenth century. *Grammar*, as it was taught in Tudor grammar schools, was not English but Latin. What's more, it was unrelenting. By the age of seven or so, children would have learnt their letters at dame school or petty school. After that, girls were taught at home, if at all, while the sons of parents who could afford to support them generally went on to the grammar school until they were fourteen. There, all day long, inky-fingered schoolboys translated Latin into English and English into Latin, memorising passages along the way. The 'small Latin'

Ben Jonson ascribed to Shakespeare would have been large by our standards.

And it stuck. The authorities made some concessions to the age of the young linguists. Among the texts chosen for them to work on were a Latin version of Aesop's *Fables*, Ovid's fast-moving tales of miraculous transformation in the *Metamorphoses* and Virgil's *Aeneid*. The *Aeneid* in particular had everything: heroic warriors, the Trojan horse, loyalty, love, sex, loss and a visit to the world of the dead. Shakespeare consistently drew on his education and not only in the plots of the plays; his reading is woven through the language he writes. 'Arion on a dolphin's back' comes from Aesop; Prospero's repudiation of magic (aka Shakespeare's farewell to the stage) paraphrases Ovid; Virgil's lovelorn Dido is mentioned in *Titus Andronicus*, *2 Henry VI*, *Romeo and Juliet*, *The Merchant of Venice*, *Hamlet*, *Antony and Cleopatra* and *The Tempest*, although the frequency of her appearances may also owe something to the influence of Christopher Marlowe's play *Dido, Queen of Carthage*, another instance of Virgil-with-a-difference.

The choice of school texts was aimed at inculcating a knowledge of pure, classical Latin and an awareness of the rhetorical skills that Roman writers took for granted. Exemplary eloquence was the criterion of selection. The children were not only learning stories; they were also acquiring style, including persuasive figures of speech and linguistic patterns. They read in order to imitate the best models, not to practise what we might recognise as criticism.

In the long run, Shakespeare evidently put his schooling to good use. But what made him influential then and now was above all his command of English. This was a moment when shared classical languages were giving way all over Europe to vernacular exchange. As well as the classics, fiction writers turned to their own national heritage: two centuries after his poetry was written, Chaucer took on a new lease of life as what Edmund Spenser called a 'well of English undefiled'. Shakespeare's Troilus and Cressida acknowledge Chaucer's Troilus and Criseyde; his Theseus in *A Midsummer Night's Dream* takes account of Chaucer's *Knight's Tale*, a story soon to be rewritten for the stage with John Fletcher as *Two Noble Kinsmen*.

Shakespeare's extensive knowledge of English fiction owed nothing to his schooling but, as time went on, examples of writing in English gradually made their way into the curriculum. If literacy was a mark of respectability, style and judgement were accomplishments. In the eighteenth century, the magnificently named Rev. Vicesimus Knox assured his readers that 'English undoubtedly ought to form a great part of an English gentleman's education'. Merchants, too, this headmaster conceded, if they were to enjoy the money they made, needed well-stocked minds and good taste. But English should not come before Latin. Boys should begin with the Greek and Roman classics, graduating to English composition by the age of thirteen or so in order not to disgrace themselves in later life by grammatical or spelling errors. In due course, they might be encouraged to model their own manner on such writers as Shakespeare, Milton, Pope and Addison, taking proper account of the beauties and defects of their respective styles. Books started to appear designed for schoolroom reading, anthologies of 'elegant extracts' for the children to emulate. Knox's own collection included Hamlet rallying the players and Brutus addressing the Romans in the marketplace.

Following the Industrial Revolution, when manufacturing and commerce began to need armies of clerks, book-keepers and invoicers, the English classics made their way into the elementary schools too. Once again, the primary project was not criticism but literacy and, in due course, composition. The children of Victorian Lark Rise took it in turns to read aloud from the *Royal Reader*, which included extracts from the novels of Sir Walter Scott, Fenimore Cooper and Washington Irving, as well as 'Young Lochinvar', 'The brook' and 'Ring out, wild bells'. Laura, fictional stand-in for the writer, soon knew them all off by heart and, since the author of *Lark Rise to Candleford* grew up to compose a bestseller, the unpromising practice evidently did its job in her case, instilling a love of books that would never leave her.

Discussion of fiction was likely to centre on grammar as the basis of writing. At her elementary school in York in 1877–8, ten-year-old Minnie Bulmer was required to copy out an excerpt from Wordsworth's 'We are seven'. Her analysis of the poem followed: 'A simple child': subject; 'draws': predicate; 'its breath': completion; 'that lightly': extension. The method continues through 'It', 'feels', 'its life', and on for two and a half verses. Minnie was given nine out of ten for this exercise. Skills developed in the process enabled her to produce a composition rehearsing the story of a virtuous emperor who rewarded a man for his wise sayings.

The stated purpose of education in English only gradually

concedes the option of reading for pleasure. Despite the best efforts of such reformers as Matthew Arnold in his role of school inspector, compulsory schooling then, as now, favoured the three Rs. The requirement for children to go to school began in Prussia in 1763. In America, Massachusetts led the way in 1852, while a Scottish Education Act of 1872 compelled school attendance. England and Wales followed suit in 1880, and fiction was there to promote reading and writing.

It was not until the twentieth century that books officially became the material for anything we might call criticism. When, after the upheaval of the First World War, the content of the curriculum came under new scrutiny, the British government set up a series of committees to make recommendations on the content of education, including

The reading lesson: Edward Henry Lamson, *A Country Schoolroom*, 1890

one on the teaching of English in England. This was chaired by Sir Henry Newbolt, whose refrain 'Play up! play up! and play the game' had previously confirmed that wars were won on the sports fields of the British independent schools. The Newbolt Report of 1921 has been pilloried for its fond belief that better English lessons could be relied on to dissolve class divisions, and there is room for doubt about whether the main aspiration of committee members was to share out the advantages of literacy more equally or to forestall social unrest by offering access to the representation of orthodox values. After all, the Russian Revolution of 1917 was very recent history. Perhaps the humane ideal was closely linked with practical politics: there remains to this day a high correlation between illiteracy and crime. Either way, the Report insisted that all children merited access to their own language and culture. By now, there was no doubt that English ought to precede Latin. Moreover, it should include the inculcation of taste, developing the 'appreciation' of good writing for its own sake. The task of the English teacher was 'first, to teach the pupil to speak and write clearly, forcibly and correctly; secondly, to foster a love of literature'.

Whether coincidentally or not, in 2014 the British government prescribed the same priorities for children in England, and in the same order. 'The overarching aim of English in the national curriculum', it declared, 'is to promote high standards of language and literacy by equipping pupils with a strong command of the spoken and written language'. Pupils will also 'develop their love of literature through widespread reading for enjoyment'. The statutory national curriculum for primary schools emphasises comprehension and vocabulary, as well as awareness of grammatical structures, while allowing that the children might begin to think about plot and style. All this, it adds, can be drawn on in their own writing.

TASTE

Appreciation, the love of literature, entailed selection. Remarkably enough, in 1921 the Newbolt Report was willing to acknowledge the role of popular fiction in introducing children to the pleasures of reading. Once they enjoy books, it confidently declares, the teacher will soon be able 'to wean them from the merely mawkish or bloodcurdling' to more wholesome fare. But in general, since fiction was included in order to provide models of style and eloquence, it should be carefully chosen. Matthew Arnold had already commented on the poor quality of the poetry reproduced in the reading books. Children deserved better. Indeed, they were entitled to what he called the best that has been thought and said in the world: Gray's 'Elegy Written in a Country Churchyard', perhaps, and extracts from Shakespeare. And so we come back to value judgements. Of course good models should be used; self-evidently, it was no use giving children badly written works to imitate. Instead, those equipped to choose for them must single out the best. And so, willy-nilly, even elementary education comes to reinforce the isolation of a canon of literature.

No harm in that, we might think: it is clear that certain works stand the test of time. In practice, however, it's not quite that simple. The Enlightenment admired Shakespeare but believed he lacked discipline: the plays were not good enough as they stood but needed rewriting to measure up to current expectations. Thereafter, his own words gradually restored, Shakespeare himself was to remain a staple of the curriculum, but other work comes and goes. In the eighteenth century Vicesimus Knox added Milton, Pope and Addison. A century later, however, Addison was to sink from view, while Dickens had become highly visible. A London County Council list of reading books popular with elementary schools in 1921 included fairy tales and fables, stories from Shakespeare, Chaucer and Spenser, *Robinson Crusoe*, *Gulliver's Travels*, and a good deal of Dickens, especially the novels involving children. Scott's *Ivanhoe* was another favourite. Scott would shortly find himself on the way out, however, along with Spenser, while metaphysical poetry and Jacobean drama were ushered in under the influence of T. S. Eliot. Eliot and F. R. Leavis between them put paid to Milton's appeal: readers of Milton are now rare outside the universities – and not always to be counted on inside them.

There are good historical reasons why fashions change, but the effect is to call into question the idea of literature as a body of timeless classics. As far as the schools are concerned, however, the consequence of canonical thinking is the early – and perhaps silent – inculcation of the assumption that there are two kinds of reading matter: works of value and the others, 'mawkish and bloodcurdling' as they might be. Although criticism is not the object of the exercise, although young children will barely learn to practise it, if at all, invisible authorities will prescribe their reading matter in advance. As a result, with the best of intentions, the field of fiction is divided by the preferences of the generation in charge: on the one hand, the books rated at that moment as literature; on the other, popular culture, best left behind at the earliest opportunity.

Taste, in other words, was taught. And what went for children also went for adult education, especially when this was addressed to an aspiring middle class. Here the dissenting academies played an early role. When the Act of Uniformity of 1662 excluded all but members of the Anglican Church from Oxford and Cambridge, non-conformists set up their own educational establishments, often more progressive and better disciplined than the universities themselves. Acquaintance with the best authors was encouraged as a foundation of social success. Meanwhile, as the Act of Union in 1707 promoted further intellectual and commercial exchange between England and Scotland, the Scots found a motive for learning to emulate admired writers of English. In mid-eighteenth-century Edinburgh, lectures by the economist Adam Smith, which appealed in the first instance to would-be merchants, singled out (the Irish) Jonathan Swift as a model of clarity and structure. Edinburgh University's first professor of Rhetoric and Belles Lettres, appointed in 1762, taught Swift, Addison, Shakespeare and Milton, among others, as examples of taste and eloquence.

In addition, literary and philosophical societies put on lectures for the general public, some of them by such critics as Coleridge and Hazlitt, while Victorian mechanics' institutes pursued similar aims for the workers attracted to them in the first instance by opportunities to develop their skills. In the 1890s, the teenage Laura, finding she had read everything her employer had to offer, joined the Candleford Mechanics Institute library and worked her way through Jane Austen, Dickens and Trollope. Others would go on to encounter the approved works thanks to the Workers' Educational Association or extra-mural evening classes.

MORALITY

All this time, it went (almost) without saying that the stylistic models put before young and old also promoted high moral standards. In the preface to the 1784 edition, Knox explained what youthful readers had to gain from the use of his *Elegant Extracts*:

> a great improvement in the English language; together with ideas on many pleasing subjects of taste and literature; and, which is of much higher importance, they will imbibe with an increase of knowledge, the purest principles of virtue and religion.

The declared purpose of the first professor of English at London University (later University College London) in 1828 was 'to inculcate lessons of virtue, through the medium of the masters of our language'.

Victorian promoters of English teaching consistently urged the moral influence of good authors. In 1800 most secondary schoolteachers were members of the clergy; by 1870 the numbers had dropped to just over half, but piety remained a crucial component of the curriculum. Studying English would make people better. From the beginning, the desire to instil virtue had its pragmatic side: education was a bulwark against crime and pauperism, both of them threats to stability and prosperity. Every kind of idleness and vice pervaded the world outside the educational institution; inside it, virtuous exertion would fortify the vulnerable against temptation, and the habit of good reading would help them withstand the influence of a histrionic press and vulgar fiction.

Indeed, as the received truths of Christianity began to falter under the combined pressures of evolutionary theory and biblical scholarship, the right books stood ready to take their moral – and spiritual – place. Matthew Arnold, who saw the alternative to culture as anarchy, fused a pragmatic purpose with the sublime. Culture, he maintained, is not reducible to politics; it is more than morality; culture is a spiritual condition, access to the 'sweetness and light' that characterises our best self. It offers an ideal that rises above petty allegiances, 'united, impersonal, at harmony' with ourselves and the world. As a school inspector, Arnold insisted that education must 'form' children through 'familiarity with masterpieces'. As a critic, he maintained that poetry was a source of solace and inspiration:

> The future of poetry is immense, because in poetry, where it is worthy of its high destinies, our race, as time goes on, will find an ever surer and surer stay ... More and more mankind will discover that we have to turn to poetry to interpret life for us, to console us, to sustain us. Without poetry, our science will appear incomplete; and most of what now passes

with us for religion and philosophy will be replaced by poetry ... But if we conceive thus highly of the destinies of poetry, we must also set our standard for poetry high, since poetry, to be capable of fulfilling such high destinies, must be poetry of a high order of excellence.

I have quoted Arnold's own words from 'The Study of Poetry' partly because no paraphrase could do justice to the rhetorical skill that lends plausibility to what is on the face of it an extraordinary claim. If poetry will supplant religion, as Arnold proposes, it follows that criticism will take the place of the sermon, and his cadences perfectly mimic the best strategies of the pulpit. The message is brought home by the simplicity of the vocabulary, emphatic reiteration of the key words (poetry, high, destinies) and the inclusion of clerical turns of phrase (surer stay, passes with us). The role of poetry, to comfort and restore, echoes the responsibility of God as the good shepherd of Psalm 23.

And how gratifying for us, as humble toilers in the vineyard (I too can be biblical), to recognise in our otherwise routine jobs as teachers, school inspectors, chairs of education committees, a proximity to the divine. The Newbolt Report of 1921, designed with this group of readers in mind, had a high regard for Arnold and quoted him extensively. Like Arnold, the committee was in many respects humane and liberal, if always with a similar eye to the risk of disorder arising from widespread illiteracy. But in among subdued discussions of organisation and pay, even while sensibly advising teachers not to overdo the grammar lessons and to bring drama into the classroom, the Report unexpectedly veers off at intervals towards a vocabulary that reaffirms the quasi-religious role of English teaching. 'Salvation' lies in healing the breach between culture and common life; professors of English are 'missionaries', while literature is not only a 'means of grace', but also 'one of the chief temples of the human spirit, in which all should worship'.

Although most English departments would now regard such rhetoric as overblown, the impulse to treat approved fiction as a source of spiritual guidance has by no means gone away. This was the imperative that drove critics to find instruction in 'A slumber did my spirit seal', where others might find only the sorrow of loss. Perhaps the clerical role is irresistible to teachers: we are offering our charges, it implies, not only an introduction to the pleasures of reading, not only an understanding of what language can do, but lessons on life. What is more, we shall decide which fictions offer the truest, most valuable preparation for living well. Such mastery is extraordinarily seductive. Underpaid, overworked and disregarded we teachers may be, but Arnold and his successors give us the illusion that we are redeeming a fallen world.

Teachers needed to be trained not just to teach but to teach English. As the nineteenth century wore on, more university courses included an element of English and in 1859 London University established a full BA in the subject. Oxbridge dragged its feet but finally, in 1894, after much controversy, Oxford established an Honours School of English Language and Literature. There was widespread fear that the new degree would be perceived as a soft option – after all, most of the works on the syllabus had been produced to give pleasure, not as objects of study. But a substantial element of Anglo-Saxon and Middle English could be relied on to stiffen the sinews. When Cambridge followed suit in 1917, however, the option of tracing English back to its Germanic origins had less appeal to a generation of students returning from the First World War. At Cambridge it was possible to be awarded an honours degree without tackling any writing before Chaucer. More, perhaps, by chance than intent, Cambridge filled the disciplinary gap with ethics.

I. A. RICHARDS

Inevitably, the first professoriate had been trained in other disciplines. I. A. Richards, appointed in 1919 from a background in moral philosophy, was determined to teach his students how to read – and read well. In his hands, criticism as an academic discipline had explicitly arrived. Richards took for granted that the right works were a storehouse of moral value and his *Principles of Literary Criticism* (1924) draws on psychology to explain why. Individuals, the book maintains, are driven by impulses, either appetites or aversions. Such random responses to stimuli are in need of organisation: 'the fine conduct of life springs only from fine ordering of responses'; 'no life can be excellent in which the elementary responses are disorganized and confused'. Works of art are made up of experiences like any other, but the fact that we know them to be works of art places the experiences at one remove, permitting us to rescue from confusion the impulses they portray or promote. Every experience, every response to a stimulus, leaves behind an imprint, and the critic's role is to distinguish valuable experiences from those that reinforce conventional attitudes. Stock responses offer no benefits: only genuine engagement with art changes us, reorders our minds.

Despite this quasi-scientific analysis, the familiar religious vocabulary makes its way back in from time to time. 'Bad taste and crude responses are not mere flaws … They are actually a root evil from which other defects follow'. And the source of this evil? Throughout the nineteenth century voices had been raised against what was increasingly perceived as an abuse of literacy, the mass circulation of cheap, formulaic fiction and sensationalist newsprint. Now there were new dangers, most notably film and radio: 'we have not yet fathomed the more sinister potentialities of the cinema and the loudspeaker', Richards warned. Mediocrity encourages stock responses, leaving people immature; only the cultivation of the highest standards can counteract the relentless debasement of reading habits, bringing mental health to the nation at large.

Original, modern (his theory of mind combines Freud with behaviourism) and ready to ask the big questions, I. A. Richards (1893–1979) dazzled post-war Cambridge. He is also often credited with the institutionalisation of close reading. *Practical Criticism* (1929) assessed the readings made by students of poems distributed without authors or dates, and the practice became a standard part of the Cambridge English curriculum.

F. R. LEAVIS

Among the most dedicated of Richards's disciples, F. R. Leavis would go on to exert an influence that spread well beyond the universities and into secondary education. Teaching was a vocation, a crusade against the mass media and the immaturity fostered by 'auto-responses'. Criticism develops taste and sensibility, he believed, equipping readers to resist the mass production of goods and emotions in a world where vulgar sentimentality too readily stands in for genuine feeling. Leavis did not reproduce Richards's arcane psychological theories. Instead, he appealed directly to *experience* itself: fiction depicts intimate experiences that we recognise from our own experience; the author 'places' the experiences of the characters, judges them in such a way that they prove instructive for the reader; characters and readers both learn from experience and each achieves maturity in the process.

F. R. Leavis, 1895–1978. Editor, with his wife Q. D. Leavis, of the widely circulated quarterly journal *Scrutiny* (1932–53). *New Bearings in English Poetry* (1932) aligned Leavis with modernism. Some of his most convincing practical criticism can be seen in *Revaluation: Tradition and Development in English Poetry* (1936). Other influential books included *The Common Pursuit* (1952) and *D. H. Lawrence: Novelist* (1955).

Maturity is highly selective: only the very best works deliver it. 'The great English novelists are Jane Austen,

George Eliot, Henry James, and Joseph Conrad – to stop for the moment at that comparatively safe point in history'. This opening sentence of *The Great Tradition* goes some way to show why Leavis secured such a following. Clear, unequivocal and resonant, it challenges woolly-minded inclusiveness: there is no space for ifs and buts; we see exactly where we are expected to stand. And the narrow ground is sharply demarcated: eat your hearts out, admirers of the also-rans, Sterne and Fielding, the Brontës or Hardy. The historical qualification will in due course allow in the contemporary D. H. Lawrence but not Virginia Woolf.

Leavis's chosen novelists 'are all distinguished by a vital capacity for experience, a kind of reverent openness before life'. That final monosyllable resounds through Leavis's writing and its connotations are once again ultimately religious. 'Life' is a highly valued term in the Bible, from the tree of life in the Garden of Eden to the river of the water of life in the book of Revelation. In the New Testament 'the letter killeth, but the spirit giveth life' (2 Corinthians 3:6), while the bread of heaven gives life to the world (John 6:33). In Leavis's secular appropriation of biblical vocabulary, the tradition of felt life holds back the dead hand of commerce and standardisation.

As *The Great Tradition* will go on to make evident, certain passages even from the chosen four novelists do not do justice to life. Discrimination is all – and discrimination is the work of the critic. While the author is responsible for placing the experiences depicted, the critic's responsibility is to place the author's placings. Criticism at once appeals to and shapes the reader's own experience. If English is a training of sensibility, the critic must be possessed of the utmost delicacy and tact, as he or she guides the reader towards increased maturity.

THE AUTHOR

In the work of Leavis, criticism as an independent practice has come to fulfil all Arnold's hopes for it. A canon of the best that has been thought and said in the world has taken the place of religion, while criticism has become the source and guardian not only of virtue but of life itself. Evaluation and ethics converge in the work of the critic.

Moreover, they find a focus in the mind of the author, whose own sensibility and maturity are conveyed by the work. Since the name of the author has conventionally demarcated a body of writing, there has long been room for a slippage between author and work: *Shakespeare* identifies a collection of plays and poems; *Shakespeare* names a once living, breathing playwright, who had (no doubt) views on the world he knew. When the biography of the artist began to be seen as a key to the work, it came to seem obvious that the work, in turn, gave direct access to the artist's thinking. And the value of the work guaranteed the value of the thoughts. In the course of the nineteenth century, the assumption took root that in reading good fiction, children were encountering the author. The 1921 Newbolt Report promoted English as 'a means of contact with great minds, a channel by which to draw upon their experience with profit and delight'. I. A. Richards held that the arts were the supreme form of communication. If the work does justice to the experience of the writer, it will arouse similar experiences in the reader.

Such communication was independent of time and place. Since universal human nature was their theme, artists spoke directly across the centuries. In 1907 Professor Walter Raleigh ascribed to Shakespeare 'a wide acquaintance with human life and human passion'. Moreover, it was a prerequisite for the playwright's critics that they were capable of participating in this knowledge. In this way a gratifying bond was established between author and commentator. As F. D. Maurice put it in 1874, the best criticism 'delights to draw forth the sense and beauty of a book ... because the heart of the critic is in sympathy with the heart of the writer'. Author and critic were partners in the exposition of human nature and the promotion of redemptive values.

ALTERNATIVES

And so, hand in hand with the professional practice of criticism in some respects, proceeding by different routes in others, education arrives at the three familiar convictions: the task in hand is evaluation, what is valued is an ethical or spiritual view of life, and that view, made available by reading, is the property of the author. In the process, ironically, fiction is no longer valued for its fictional qualities. Instead, it is effectively reduced to assessable, moral, biographical fact.

Although some of the earlier rhetoric has come to seem

extravagant, similar attitudes remain widespread. Even if the canon has broadened in recent years to include works that Leavis would have held beneath contempt, some members of English departments still isolate literature from other fiction without hesitation. Literature is the respectable stuff, not only well written but morally improving. The American philosopher Martha Nussbaum and others still insist that democratic education must continue to include the civilising influence of carefully selected fiction. Meanwhile, biographies of authors are the nearest many bookstores come to stocking anything that could pass for criticism.

In among the regular pieties of the English department, however, other possibilities have made themselves audible. For one, historicism interprets writing in the context of its own time. We cannot do justice to the work, historicists maintain, without some grasp of its setting. But once interpretation appeals to history, once the particularity of the past enters into the reading process, universal human nature finds itself less firmly grounded. If fiction speaks across the centuries, perhaps it does so with the effect of testifying to historical difference and the possibility of change.

Second, in order to denounce contemporary popular culture effectively, critics found themselves attending to it more closely than they had expected. And while modernity was often unmasked as radically inadequate by comparison with a lost golden past, in due course some critics would come to see traces of this past in the popular material of the present. Traditional features of working-class culture were seen to have value, after all, if in slightly less elevated terms.

On this basis the distinct discipline of cultural studies was born, for better or worse.

HISTORICISM

First, the emergence of historicism. From the outset, the University of Oxford taught the English degree on historical lines, tracing fiction from its roots in Anglo-Saxon epic and elegiac poetry, through Middle English storytelling and lyric verse, to somewhere just short of any given present. An examination paper on the history of the language required students to grasp changes of meaning and usage. I remember learning how the flowers that wept in *A Midsummer Night's Dream*, 'lamenting some enforced chastity', were mourning rape, not compulsory celibacy. Incidental as it seems, this instance records the value, held in high esteem in the past, and indeed in some current cultures, of virginity as a property of marriageable young women. *Rape*, meanwhile, was derived from the Latin for *theft*. Victims of rape were not only violated; they and their families had their prized chastity stolen in the process.

This example has stayed in my mind, but there were others. The meanings of major terms, *reason* and *nature*, for instance, have shifted over time, and the record of the changes offers the material of a social and cultural history. *Criticism*, too, has a story (the one I have set out to tell). Its earliest recorded occurrences in English were concerned with judgement, usually negative. In 1683 *The Art of Converse* called criticism 'a censorious humour, condemning indifferently everything'. That general sense survives but, at about the same time, *criticism* took on the specific role of judging works of art. While the emergence of civil society in the long eighteenth century involved the establishment of standards to measure gentility, taste and discernment, much subsequent reflection on criticism has been devoted to widening the meaning of the word.

For example, if *criticism* offers an overarching term for the work of English departments, historicism was one mode of analysis that offered an escape from the relentless compulsion to judge. As early as 1848, for example, in his inaugural lecture at University College London, Professor A. J. Scott pondered the question of how English, or any vernacular literature, could justify academic study. Poets, he concluded, were the voice of their time, and their time in turn makes itself evident in their work. Cromwell and Galileo were implicit in *Paradise Lost*; understanding Shakespeare fully requires a sense of 'the phraseology, customs, incidents, outward life' of his age. To study the 'mind' of a people, we should read their poetry.

Scott's far-sighted vision was not entirely fulfilled. While Oxford fostered an awareness of history most notably in the work of C. S. Lewis, whose *Discarded Image* sketched the shared assumptions of the Middle Ages, Cambridge produced E. M. W. Tillyard, whose *Elizabethan World Picture* became a bestseller. From the perspective of a modern-day historicist, both these writers had their limitations. If Lewis tended to see medieval culture as a prelude to the Anglican Church, Tillyard longed for a world where social unrest was unthinkable because everyone knew their place. He found this happy hierarchy in early modern England, where he claimed it was promoted by an arch-conservative Shakespeare. Tillyard could hardly have been more wrong on either count but his story proved remarkably tenacious.

And then in 1980 a new book took English departments by storm. Stephen Greenblatt's *Renaissance Self-Fashioning* located a succession of sixteenth-century writers in an authoritarian society where their survival depended on shaping their own identities in accordance with expectation. These identities were not simply given but constructed within and in response to the prevailing culture. Greenblatt's early modern society was no longer Tillyard's golden world: on the contrary, social relations were defined by the ruthless exercise of power. American English departments, recognising something of their own political present in Greenblatt's Tudor England, and tired of four decades of New Criticism (of which more in chapter 4), fell instantly in love with this eloquent, sophisticated analysis and turned themselves over to New Historicism in record time.

Stephen Greenblatt, b. 1943. As Professor of English at Berkeley and then Harvard, he followed *Renaissance Self-Fashioning* most notably with *Shakespearean Negotiations* (1988), *Learning to Curse: Essays in Early Modern Culture* (1990) and his prize-winning *The Swerve* (2011). He has also published a bestselling biography of Shakespeare, *Will in the World* (2004).

New Historicism too has its limitations. The anthropology that went into construing the setting proved so fascinating, the chosen records from the epoch so well lit, that the fictional works themselves tended to fade by comparison. The problem is readily apparent in James Shapiro's bestselling *1599: A Year in the Life of William Shakespeare*, published in 2005. There the context of Shakespeare's writing is vividly depicted, the political struggles of the time are richly brought to life, but the plays remain much as the Victorians left them.

My own vision of what historicism might do is different. Rather than look outside fiction itself for confirmation of what we find there, 'background' reinforcing 'foreground', we might treat the fictional works themselves as the material of a distinctive kind of cultural history. There will be more to say about that in chapter 5.

CULTURAL STUDIES

Meanwhile, another kind of cultural analysis was emerging. Foremost among the critics of Victorian values, Matthew Arnold, like many of his contemporaries, looked at his society and found it wanting. He saw the middle class as driven not only by greed but by an earnest and mindless adherence to a narrowly defined morality. Arnold called them Philistines. In his view, the aristocracy were no help. Emanating sweetness but not light, setting the standard of good manners but inflexible and autocratic, dedicated to physical prowess at the expense of the soul, they deserved to be seen as Barbarians. To his mind, the solution was *culture* as the best that had been thought and said. But in making his case, Arnold was inadvertently offering an analysis of his *culture* understood in a quite different sense: the values and attitudes that define a society. He was looking at his own community, if somewhat cursorily, in the way an anthropologist views the rituals, customs and utterances of another culture.

At the time, popular culture, the material available to people at large, remained generally beneath the gaze of subscribers to the view that literature offered an encounter with great minds. But in due course those who denounced the decline of mass culture found themselves looking for examples of its degeneracy. In *Culture and Environment* (1933), their practical manual for teachers, Leavis and the schoolmaster Denys Thompson not only paid attention to the cultural practices they deplored, but recommended their inclusion in the English curriculum. Even while disparaging wireless and cinema (as well as motor coaches and cars), and vilifying advertising and the press, they drew attention to specific effects the media were designed to bring about. The book points out, for example, that consumerism depends on creating fear about whether we measure up, a pervasive anxiety that can be allayed only by buying more things. In addition, they saw 'highbrow', then evidently a buzzword, as dangerous because it set out to distinguish literature from the works accessible to ordinary people.

True, the exercises on popular culture that Leavis and Thompson proposed for students mostly required them to illustrate foregone and negative conclusions, rather than to judge for themselves, but the essay questions set in the book might be seen as the seeds of a more exploratory analysis of contemporary culture.

Leavis and Thompson found an alternative to a mass-produced modernity in an organic, rural past of cottages and unalienated labour, of 'time-honoured ways of living and the inherited wisdom of the folk'. Never mind that this golden world also included regular bread riots, high levels of vagrancy and the ruthless policing of deviance by the community itself. To its adherents it represented an ideal of order and well-being. But in Britain after the World War of 1939–45, times were changing. Leavis's successors included figures who were less convinced by the story of an organic, communitarian past but were willing to find in traditional working-class culture itself values to counteract individualist consumerism. Richard Hoggart looked back with nostalgia to his childhood in Leeds; Raymond Williams invoked the mutual support fostered by cooperatives, friendly societies and trade unions.

If they were responding to social change, Hoggart and Williams were also engaging in a battle for the meaning and role of culture itself: on their part, a desire to engage with the context, defining *culture* in inclusive terms; on the other, a determined effort to keep the context at bay, confining *culture* to the so-called timeless classics. Like the First World War, the Second World War entailed a new social mobility. Recession in the 1930s had already politicised intellectual debate; now, established hierarchies were under practical threat. Tillyard was doing his best to maintain the existing order: his celebration of respect for rank in *The Elizabethan World Picture* was published in 1943. A year later, he extended the campaign with *Shakespeare's History Plays*. But it was already too late: the populist die was cast. In 1944 a new Education Act made attendance at a grammar school free to any child in England and Wales judged capable of benefiting from it, and social relations were irreversibly on the move.

Tillyard was not alone in his anxiety. T. S. Eliot was deeply disturbed by the thought that state education might now be the means of transmitting culture from one generation to another. Instead, he believed, the preservation of the best depended on an elite minority who could be relied on to inherit good taste, pass on the tradition and patronise what was most valuable in the present. In *Notes Towards the Definition of Culture*, published in 1948, Eliot concedes that what is valuable might be surprisingly widely understood, to include the cup final as well as Henley Regatta, Wensleydale cheese in addition to the music of Elgar. Such things, he allows, make life worth living. But at its heart culture *cultivates*, improves on what is given by nature; it puts before us an ideal to aspire to.

T. S. Eliot, 1888–1965, poet, playwright and critic, declared himself a royalist in politics and an Anglo-Catholic in religion. *The Waste Land* (1922) was recognised as a landmark of modernism; he himself saw *Four Quartets* (1936–42) as his masterpiece. *Murder in the Cathedral* (1935) was his most successful play.

Eliot's *Notes* set out, as the title indicates, to define *culture*. The meaning of the term was in the balance. On the one hand, the anthropological sense includes all the beliefs and practices of a society; on the other, the traditional meaning confines *culture* to the best. Eliot's book defends the traditional meaning – but includes a trace of the anthropological sense.

Ten years later in *Culture and Society*, Raymond Williams took the opposite view, favouring the anthropological meaning – but with a trace of tradition. *Culture* was ordinary, everyday, the whole way of life of a people. Minority privilege endangered social well-being. 'We need a common culture, not for the sake of an abstraction, but because we shall not survive without it.' The idea of improvement had not gone away, however. The 'whole' way of life we must share was also 'wholesome', healthy; it would make us 'whole'.

Raymond Williams, 1921–88. The son of a railway signalman, Williams was educated at Abergavenny Grammar School and Cambridge. After starting his academic career in adult education, he moved to the University of Cambridge in 1961. Consistently polemical, always influential, his work included *The Long Revolution* (1961), *Modern Tragedy* (1966), *The Country and the City* (1973) and *Keywords* (1976), as well as the novel *Border Country* (1960).

Working-class culture was also the theme of Richard Hoggart's passionate, personal account of *The Uses of Literacy* in 1957. Debasement by the media had been overstated, he argued; working-class values were able to put up at least some resistance to the best efforts of journalism, pulp fiction and advertising to consolidate mindless consumerism.

But he identified as a particular threat the populist anti-intellectualism promoted by an anonymous, commercialised culture, and especially by those columnists in the press who pandered to the prejudice of 'the plain man' in 'syndicated ordinariness for the millions'. Newspapers, magazines and fiction sold copies by confirming the shallowest version of the received wisdom.

Richard Hoggart, 1918–2014, owed his education to scholarships and began his academic career in adult education. In addition to *The Uses of Literacy*, he published a good deal of cultural criticism, including *Auden* (1951) and *The Way We Live Now: Dilemmas in Contemporary Culture* (1995).

The Uses of Literacy attends closely to the cultural practices it fears. In 1961 Hoggart was appointed to a Chair in English at Birmingham University and, under his aegis, the Centre for Contemporary Cultural Studies opened three years later. The consequences were far-reaching but ambiguous. On the one hand, judgements of value were no longer the primary purpose of attention to fiction. In cultural studies, critical discussion was more likely to centre on how popular storytelling worked: the emotions it appealed to, the attitudes it promoted, the effects it might have. Details, hitherto ignored because they did not belong to great art, would now become topics of analysis; stereotypes were not dismissed but studied. Among many early examples, it was noted that at the time black actors rarely appeared in classic Hollywood films outside service or entertainment roles; westerns conventionally depicted Native Americans as the enemy; romantic comedy defined happiness as heterosexual marriage. The influence of the new discipline was far-reaching: these days there is no need to be a cultural studies graduate to spot examples of everyday sexual and racial stereotyping.

While the analysis grew a good deal more subtle, however, the field of culture was now more sharply fractured than ever, its division cemented institutionally. For a decade or more, English was left to its conventional devices, extracting moral worth from encounters with great minds in literary works that spanned the centuries, while cultural studies would focus mainly on the present – and on everything that was left behind by literature. To the extent that this promoted serious critical analysis of film, radio, television, the press and, in due course, the internet, that could only be welcome. In so far as it confirmed the divide between literature and the rest of fiction, however, it stood to damage intellectual enquiry, cutting off the formula romances from their roots in *Pride and Prejudice* and *Jane Eyre*, say, or severing popular song from lyric poetry. Cultures are full of fine differences but these distinctions are not more visible in the light of a single, binary division.

In the event, the influence of cultural studies on English itself, in conjunction with social and intellectual developments in the 1970s, would radically expand the English curriculum too. And both disciplines would be transformed by the advent of theory. That story, however, deserves a chapter of its own.

4

THE ROLE OF THEORY

'SOME MUTE INGLORIOUS MILTON'

Is theory compatible with a rich, intense involvement in reading? Some would say not, but it underpins the work of criticism even so. Theory is no more, in the end, than reflection on what critics do. Any practice of criticism takes – or takes for granted – a position on the relationship between language and the writer, as well as between representation and the world. And no assumption is more pervasive than that writers *use* language to *communicate* an idea or a view of reality. But do they? Much recent thinking has called that common-sense conviction into question and challenged in the process the conventional critical preoccupations with evaluation, morality and the author.

The view that language is a tool for communicating ideas or experiences may not be as well founded as it seems. Perhaps words are both more and less than instruments of a prior intention. Certainly, the process of representation has long made itself felt as an issue in some eminently respectable places. Gray's 'Elegy Written in a Country Churchyard', recommended by Matthew Arnold for use in schools, proposes that the main source of writing is other writing. Gray's poem speculates that among the dead in the rural graveyard there lies 'Some mute inglorious

Milton', an unacknowledged because wordless poet. The roughly carved monuments and modest epitaphs register the limited literacy of the agricultural poor at the time. In different circumstances, with the advantages of education, the villagers might have made their names in the world as legislators or writers.

The poem is ambivalent about their lot: if these people did not achieve fame, at least the harm they could do was confined to the neighbourhood. What must have appealed most strongly to the school inspector in Arnold, however, was the explanation of the country Milton's silence. At its conclusion, the poem imagines an old man inviting a future traveller to contemplate the epitaph carved on the tombstone of the poet himself. 'Approach and read', the guide urges, 'for thou canst read'. By contrast, a barely literate rural population, who might have swayed empires or inspired others in verse, are held back by their ignorance of the written tradition: 'Knowledge to their eyes her ample page / Rich with the spoils of time did ne'er unroll'.

Thomas Gray, 1716–71. Poet and classical scholar at Cambridge University. The 'Elegy' was published in 1751, one of a handful of poems he entrusted to print.

Knowledge belongs on the page and is available to readers, while merit on its own remains mute. Genius, in other words, needs material to work on, especially the spoils appropriated from past cultures. And Milton himself, anything but mute and in so many ways Gray's own model, is not named at random. The treasures that go into the making of *Paradise Lost* include the Latin and Greek classics, as well as the Bible and the earlier English poets. As if to prove Gray's point, the Christian epic begins with a direct echo of its pagan predecessors. 'Of man's first disobedience ... Sing heavenly Muse'. On classical authority, Milton abandons the word order of native English speech for a pattern familiar

'Knowledge to their eyes her ample page / Rich with the spoils of time did ne'er unroll.'

in Latin. 'Arms and the man I sing', Virgil declares in the opening line of the *Aeneid*. And Virgil in turn invokes the first lines of Homer's *Iliad*, an appeal to the goddess of song to help the poet depict the wrath of Achilles.

If Milton's poem establishes its own genre by invoking the Greek and Roman epics, Gray's 'Elegy' quotes Milton's own elegy, *Lycidas*. Most poetry is citational. Even Wordsworth's apparently artless 'A slumber did my spirit seal' reworks with a difference, as I suggested in chapter 1, the ballad tradition, then making its way towards enthusiastic reception in a growing civil society. In addition, Wordsworth's elegy owes a debt to Gray's celebration of the nameless and unassuming dead. The Muse cannot sing without at least some sense of genre or convention. Imagine, for example, sitting down to write a novel with no idea what a novel is. However inevitable it may appear to us, this form is highly evolved, each new generation of novelists following – or, better, breaking – the genre's own complex rules. The best advice to a would-be writer is 'Read!' Without previous works to imitate, incorporate, modify or resist, Milton himself would have stayed mute and inglorious.

VOCABULARY

When it came to education, the Victorians recognised this, and prescribed reading as the basis of composition. They knew that writing required access to the rich resources of the language. Arnold's reports in his capacity as school inspector assume that reading expands intellectual horizons because it increases vocabulary. This is also a recurrent theme of the Newbolt Report of 1921. English, the Report maintains, is not just another subject but a requirement for all subjects. Without knowing what the words mean, children cannot master any discipline. What is more, a child's own ideas, lacking the definition that belongs to representation, remain hazy, inchoate and evanescent. If children cannot read, they cannot learn; if they cannot write, they cannot put to work what they have learnt. Indeed, the Report insists more than once, English is 'not merely the medium of our thought, it is the very stuff and process of it'.

But if knowledge increases with vocabulary, if the expansion of their native tongue is the condition of children's intellectual development, then language is more than an instrument that we use to express pre-existing thoughts and ideas. Instead, it has primacy, along with such other forms of representation as images and the symbols that belong to mathematics and logic. As the Newbolt Committee realised, we learn our own language and with it the meanings and values that make up our culture – in the broadest sense of that term.

This is not to deny the existence of sensations and feelings that are deep, visceral and hard to describe – unless art finds ways of characterising them. But thoughts, ideas? They are acquired. Whether or not we know what they are, it is evident that *utopia, percentages, the excluded middle, justice, parallel universes, decimals, digital teletransportation, the most recent common ancestor* and *human rights* do not in the first instance pose in the world of experience just waiting to be named. Neither, come to that, do *the music of the spheres, Martians, replicants, dragons, nymphs* or even *shepherds* as they feature in pastoral poetry. And yet we learn, sometimes very early on, what these terms mean. His play *Cocktail Sticks* imagines Alan Bennett looking in Leeds for examples of *sward*. He knew what it was from his reading: a particularly lush, thick grass, where knights could be relied on to rescue maidens in distress. But he was reluctantly compelled to conclude that there was no hope of encountering it himself: 'Leeds didn't run to sward.'

Most people's experience doesn't run to subatomic particles or dark matter, either, but it doesn't follow that we can't learn what scientists mean by them. The expansion of vocabulary gives access to what exists beyond the everyday – and what might come to exist or will remain imaginary. It also indicates the relationships between things, or between ideas, in terms that have no referents outside the world of thoughts: *because, although, despite, in so far as, notwithstanding.* Many humanities disciplines reside primarily in language. Learn the vocabulary of philosophy in such a way that you can join in a discussion between philosophers and you're doing philosophy. Come by the terminology of criticism, whether or not you choose to include 'access to great minds' and 'maturity', and you're equipped to practise criticism.

But, oddly enough, once we give language this important role, the great minds and maturity begin to fade from view. If language is not just a medium of communication between two psyches, the writer's and the reader's, but instead the very stuff and process of thought, the critic's focus shifts towards the language that composes the work.

Commentary on a piece of writing no longer depends on something seen as behind it, a prior thought, a message, a purpose; instead, it looks closely at the work to see what it says. And once the work is the object of study, what it says proves to be more elusive than before. The possibility even arises that communication isn't quite what takes place.

AMBIGUITY

Out of interwar Cambridge English, nostalgic and sanctimonious as it was, there sprang a critic who was neither. William Empson, a student of I. A. Richards, was 24 when he published *Seven Types of Ambiguity* in 1930. Clearly remarkable, Empson had been nominated for a fellowship in Cambridge, but then condoms were found in his room. Banishment followed and had he not left for the Far East, the history of criticism might have been very different. (If evidence is needed of historical change, it is surely in this story. Nowadays he might have been thought irresponsible *not* to have condoms in his room.)

The young Empson had been reading Robert Graves and, in particular, a short, polemical book Graves had published with Laura Riding in 1927 on modernist poetry. One chapter deplored the way editors modernised the punctuation of a Shakespeare sonnet, ironing out in the process alternative meanings. Graves and Riding dissected the poem in its first printed form to show distinct meanings enlisted in a 'furiously dynamic' relationship, where no single sense cancelled out the others. Although Empson did not copy this focus on punctuation, the idea that a work might not confine itself to a single transparent message evidently planted a seed.

With hindsight, the publication of *Seven Types of Ambiguity* marks the moment when the lines defining the theoretical debates of the following century become perceptible, gradually at first, before emerging into full view. On one side, traditional criticism continued to concern itself with the mind behind the work; on the other, the text (Empson tentatively uses the word) might say more than the writer knew. Meaning becomes separable from intention. Suppose Gray, for example, intended to present the plight of the poor as a melancholy but inevitable fact of life. That design would be compatible with the stoicism of the reclusive scholar, as well as with aspects of the poem. But if meaning is not the same as intention, Arnold would not be misreading when he saw the poem as delivering a challenge to that view in favour of spreading literacy. From the textual perspective, the question is what the work makes available to the reader or audience, who now begin to feature in the critical project. The job of the critic is to identify a range of options, without necessarily settling for the one, intended, *authorised* interpretation.

In that light, it is worth dwelling on the nature of Empson's intervention. Although *Seven Types* has become a classic work of criticism, it is more widely admired than read. The book is quite demanding, not on account of knotty passages or jargon but because it expects exactly the kind of reading it also prescribes. *Seven Types of Ambiguity* does not allow its readers to skip the quotations: on the contrary, extracts form the substance of the argument. Passages of text, familiar or otherwise, are printed with very little preparation or context, and the reader is invited to assent to a range of possible interpretations, none final or definitive. In my experience, it is necessary to read the quoted passage once to make it out at all, then to reread it closely, looking for the suggested ambiguities one by one. Moreover, the initial reaction is often incredulity: Empson's way of reading never settles for the obvious. But to overcome the preference for the obvious reading is to see that the extract may be more dense or suggestive than it seemed at first.

The best way, then, to characterise Empson's approach is to offer an example. Shakespeare's Macbeth has killed the king and taken his place, but he is tortured by fears and bad dreams. Now he has given instructions for the death of Banquo and Fleance that evening, and looks out of the window to see how close he is to the hour of the murder:

> Come, seeling night,
> Scarf up the tender eye of pitiful day,
> And, with thy bloody and invisible hand,
> Cancel and tear to pieces that great bond
> Which keeps me pale. Light thickens,
> And the crow makes wing to th' rooky wood;
> Good things of day begin to droop and drowse,
> Whiles night's black agents to their preys do rouse.

As Macbeth struggles to think bloodthirsty thoughts, repudiating his own humanity ('That great bond / Which keeps me pale'), 'Light thickens'. The phrase captures the deepening obscurity as the night comes on but also looks back, Empson suggests, to the witches' brew of the opening scenes. This association invokes the iniquity that makes Macbeth's observation more than a comment on the time of day, gathering up the oppositions between good and evil, light and darkness, that pervade the play and the passage. Meanwhile, 'crow' presents its own kind of puzzle. Is *crow* another word for *rook*? Is the crow, in other words, to be envied in its flight home to sleep peacefully among its fellows, as the tormented Macbeth no longer can? Or is it, conversely, a carrion crow, a solitary predator, like Macbeth himself, one of 'night's black agents', a misfit in the innocent rookery, as Macbeth is out of place among honest people? Usage of the word *crow* in the period would support either reading.

Empson indicates that we need not decide. But can we sustain more than one interpretation in our minds, without the one erasing the other? I believe we can, just as we know at a sad movie, even while we weep for the characters, that they are not real. The depth that many people find in Shakespeare may depend precisely on this dispersal of suggestion: Macbeth longs to be an unoffending rook as he nerves himself to remain a carrion crow, and so two antithetical imperatives converge in one ambiguous word. It's not so much that we choose the reading we prefer, though that is one possibility. Instead, keeping both in view at once allows the recognition that states of mind may be ambivalent, incoherent, contradictory – and that language is by nature open to more than one interpretation. In the same way, Gray's 'Elegy' might be quietist and yet leave itself open to radical interpretation at the same time.

Once again, nothing in Empson's argument suggests that

anything goes, or that any reading is as good as any other. His own interpretations may not be infallible, but the range of possible meanings he puts forward is usually justified by reference to other examples. Objectors, preferring ridicule to the hard work of following suggestion where it leads, have caricatured such approaches as encouraging us to make up whatever interpretation suits us.

Nothing could be further from the truth. But the wish to choose one meaning at the expense of all the others dies hard. It stems from our everyday assumption that language is no more than an instrument of communication. Early editors of *Macbeth* made no bones about their understanding of their task. It was to arrive at a coherent and logical version of a wayward text on the basis of the single meaning the dramatist must have had in mind. In the extract Empson quotes, they found 'rooky' particularly puzzling: it wasn't a proper word. One editor, unable to see any connection with the next line, put forward an amendment: 'I cannot ... help supposing that our author wrote – "makes wing to rook i'th'wood". That is, to *roost* in it.' Another Victorian commentator came up with an alternative possibility: 'I should imagine Sh. intended to give us the idea of the gloominess of the woods at the close of the evening, and wrote, – "to th' *murky* (or *dusky*) wood"'. Research into local dialects was adduced to justify other improvements.

Later in his book, Empson gleefully quotes the first Arden editor's emphatic rebuttal of all previous emendations in favour of his own interpretation of 'rooky' as meaning 'rouking' (perching). Simply by listing the other options, the Arden note brings them before us, Empson claims, offering us the possibility of acknowledging more than one meaning. And he adds mischievously, 'I believe the nineteenth-century editor secretly believed in a great many of his alternatives at once'.

If he did, however, he kept it to himself. And Empson's unfamiliar way of reading was slow to exert an influence. In 1951, Kenneth Muir's second Arden edition continued to list all the previous options, only to dismiss them, including his predecessor's, in favour of a no-nonsense single gloss: *rooky* means 'black and filled with rooks'. As for the crow, it's a rook, on the zoological basis that 'the carrion crow is not gregarious'. But times did eventually change. A. L. Braun-muller in the Cambridge edition of the play in 2008 thought the crow might be either a friendly rook or a predatory crow, and added the interesting suggestion that 'Light thickens' might evoke the 'fog and filthy air' of the first scene. Mean-while, Nicholas Brooke in his Oxford edition the same year quoted Empson on rooks and crows as authoritative – in a final triumph for ambiguity.

Sir William Empson, 1906–84, critic and poet. Profes-sor of English at Sheffield University 1953–71. His books include *Some Versions of Pastoral* (1935), *The Struc-ture of Complex Words* (1951) and *Milton's God* (1961). He was knighted in 1979, in the year his former Cam-bridge College, Magdalene, awarded him an honorary fellowship.

MASTERY LOST

But by that time, there had been a good many advances in thinking about language, and for the majority of its practitioners criticism had changed in consequence. What Empson had uncovered, even if inadvertently, was the way meaning slips and skids, while no one seems in total control of the wheel. In 1606, a *crow* could be a crow or a rook; Shakespeare might or might not have made a conscious choice between those options; if he did, however, no one now has any way of knowing which he chose. And, in a further possibility, even if we could ask and he gave us an answer, who is to say that the other, unconscious meaning, wasn't among the reasons why the line seemed to him to work?

How, then, can the critic construct a reliable reading? In a well-ordered world, no doubt, one word would have one meaning and only one; moreover this one meaning would be permanent. In practice, the world of language is not ordered in such a logical way. For example, in early modern English *let* can mean either *obstruct* or *permit*. (A trace of the first option survives in 'without let or hindrance'.) When Hamlet, determined to follow the Ghost whatever the danger, declares, 'I'll make a ghost of him that lets me', we diligently explain to our students that *lets* in that instance means *impedes*. But deep down we know that it might also connote *allows*, not confined to this moment but foreshadowing the hero's future as what my friend and colleague Helen Cooper wittily calls a serial killer. In the course of the play Hamlet will polish off any meddler who gives him the chance, including Polonius, Rosencrantz and Guildenstern, and indirectly Ophelia, before he finally reaches Laertes and then Claudius.

The account of language as inherently ambiguous delivered a major challenge to the mastery beloved of critics. I'm not even sure whether I believe that 'lets' has both meanings in the *Hamlet* passage. But I can't quite rule out the possibility, either. It is impossible to cling to one definitive interpretation while at the same time conceding that language lives an anarchic life of its own. The idea of unresolved ambiguity had undermined faith in the stability of a single meaning and, even if it took a while to register with some, there was in the end no going back.

MASTERY REGAINED

Among the first to get the point were the American New Critics, whose mission it was to *recuperate* ambiguity. There is no precise way of translating into English that sense of the French *récuperer*. It means to rehabilitate, harness or bring into line. New Criticism took over ambiguity and made it safe by renaming it 'paradox'. Where ambiguity leaves differences unresolved, paradox reconciles antithetical meanings and dissolves incongruities in either irony or wonder. When Pope in *An Essay on Man* defines humankind as 'The glory, jest, and riddle of the world', if the first two contradictory affirmations are justified, the paradox proclaims a single, ironic truth: at once magnificent and ridiculous, humanity is a conundrum. Equally, when Henry Vaughan asserts, 'There is in God, some say, / A deep, but dazzling darkness', the paradoxical radiance and mystery of the divine is shown to exceed mere human logic.

In *The Well Wrought Urn*, first published in 1947, the New Critic Cleanth Brooks brilliantly traced the ambiguities in a succession of works from different epochs to find a 'fusion' brought into being by the creative imagination's defiance of reason. His account of *Macbeth* ignores crows and rooks but extracts instead an earlier image from Macbeth's horrified contemplation of the projected murder:

> pity, like a naked new-born babe,
> Striding the blast, or heaven's cherubin, horsed
> Upon the sightless couriers of the air ...

Is pity to be understood here, Brooks asks, as a helpless – pitiful – baby that would surely be at the mercy of the blast, incapable of striding anywhere? Or is it an infant possessing supernatural powers, like the angels who ride the winds with confidence, but are in consequence hardly pitiable? Ingeniously tracing the baby imagery through the play, Brooks concludes triumphantly: 'It is both; and it is strong because of its very weakness. The paradox is inherent in the situation itself; and it is the paradox that will destroy the over-brittle rationalism on which Macbeth founds his career'. The critic has located a puzzle, solved it, and regained control of the work.

Where Empson had dealt in fragments, the New Critics read whole poems or verse-plays (they were not as interested in prose) in search of unity and balance. And the method lent itself readily to pedagogic practice: the class could unpick specific words and passages to find unexpected meanings that would contribute to the single, complex, paradoxical sense of the whole. New Criticism became the prevailing orthodoxy in America, while in the UK it made a dent in the old historicism and Leavisism. Eventually, however, in the 1980s New Historicism was to steal its (by then somewhat tired) thunder – and assert its own difference by echoing the name.

Cleanth Brooks, 1906–94. Professor of English at Yale University, 1947–75. Specialist in Southern fiction, especially the work of William Faulkner. *Understanding Poetry* (1938) was compiled jointly with Robert Penn Warren for classroom use. *Literary Criticism: A Short History* (1957), written with William K. Wimsatt, isn't short by normal standards.

THE CHALLENGE OF NEW CRITICISM

So much attention to the words on the page was bound to affect the previous trio of critical purposes, to establish the value, the moral and the author's intention. But it did not change them all at once or to the same degree. Evaluation remained in place but became more incidental. The fact that the works chosen for analysis repaid close attention was evidence enough of their value. New Critical preferences did not significantly challenge the canon in place at that time. Ethical instruction, similarly, was marginalised without quite going away: poetry was not an instrument of edification; moral value should not be mistaken for poetic value. Indeed, the work could be slightly misguided morally without serious damage to its standing. What mattered was the depth, complexity, subtlety and – there it is again – *maturity* of its insights into the human condition.

The author, on the other hand, was well and truly relegated. Perhaps the most influential of all the New Critics' theoretical statements was the essay by William K. Wimsatt and Monroe C. Beardsley denouncing 'The Intentional Fallacy' (1946). The design of the writer, Wimsatt and Beardsley insisted, was not available to the reader. If the author's intention had been realised in the work, it would be evident there; if not, it was irrelevant. Once again, language is seen as more than the bearer of a message from one individual to another. A poem does not belong to the author: on the contrary, the work is public property, because 'It is embodied in language, the peculiar possession of the public'. And so meaning is a matter of public access, to be discovered 'through the semantics and syntax of a poem, through our habitual knowledge of the language, through grammars, dictionaries, and all the literature which is the source of dictionaries, in general through all that makes a language and culture'.

New Criticism would never become more radical than this. If writing relies on other writing, as well as existing usage, interpretation depends on familiarity with usage and existing writing. The best advice for a would-be critic, then, resembles the advice to writers: 'Read!' Understand how words hang together, know the history of the language, familiarise yourself with the range of possible genres – and don't worry about the personality of the author.

The logic of their position impelled the New Critics to detach the 'I' of the poem from the author and, in the process, to treat the text as a work of fiction. Whatever the Romantics may have believed, however deeply felt the work, a piece of writing produced according to – or in defiance of – the prevailing constraints of meaning, form and genre, can never be simply the spontaneous overflow of powerful feelings. (It has always struck me as odd that anyone might suppose the first impulse of a person in the white heat of passion would be to give vent to that emotion by composing, say, a tightly structured 14-line poem with a complicated rhyme scheme.) The New Critics replaced the writer with a fictional stand-in who was experiencing the passion, whether or not the author shared it at that moment. 'Even a short lyric poem is dramatic, the response of a speaker ... to a situation ... We ought to impute the thoughts and attitudes of the poem immediately to the dramatic *speaker*'. And true to this principle, their commentaries ignored the author in favour of this figure that they named as voicing an utterance, or sometimes as 'the lover', or else (hedging their bets) 'the poet'.

Like Empson, the New Critics provided a tentative place for readers or audiences. The addressees of the work are expected to be alert to its ambiguities, able to grasp the paradoxes. Moreover, they now become the imagined guarantee of successful criticism: 'informed' readers will judge the value of the critic's account and, assuming they are informed in precisely the same way as the critic, they are likely to confirm the interpretation.

FRENCH THEORY

So much for the Anglo-American tradition. In Paris, meanwhile, in the wake of the Second World War, a degree of soul-searching led to a new kind of interest in language and culture. How was it that civilised Germany had allowed itself to elect, and then failed to overthrow, a government driven by such repellent convictions? How, worse, had so many citizens of occupied France been induced to collaborate with the enemy? And why, now the war was over, was social revolution so slow in coming?

The answers, certain thinkers proposed, lay in culture in the anthropological sense of the word. Culture, they believed, offers us myths to live by; representation influences the way we think. A generation of French theorists turned back with interest to an earlier book on language by Ferdinand de Saussure. What they found in the *Course in General Linguistics* (1916) were observations on the workings of language, and a vocabulary that made it possible to think of meaning in new ways.

First, words were not just labels for pre-existing ideas. Instead, by implication, they were their source. What Gray and the Victorians had intuited, what Newbolt had insisted, that language was the stuff and process of thought, Saussure now argued with examples, pointing out that different languages conceptualise the world in different ways. Saussure argued from translation, a practice that presents any number of difficulties. *Récuperer* meaning *make safe* has no precise English equivalent. Some languages have tenses not available in others: some, including French but not

English, have a special narrative tense, for example. Many languages have alternative forms of the second person: *tu / vous*; *Du / Sie*. Here the difference signifies distinct degrees of intimacy: how to capture the shift from one to the other in modern English? Conversely, while *le mouton* might be grazing in the field or ready for consumption in French, English distinguishes between *sheep* and *mutton*. As it happens, this particular difference has a history. In Caryl Churchill's *Light Shining in Buckinghamshire*, the corn merchant Star points out that Anglo-Saxon farm workers raised the live animals and French-speaking Norman aristocrats encountered them cooked and on the table.

Examples could be endlessly multiplied of differences that do not quite correspond in other tongues: translators confront them daily. The conclusion Saussure drew from this was at once obvious and startling. The ideas did not come first; language could not be the instrument of prior thoughts. 'If words stood for pre-existing concepts, they would all have exact equivalents in meaning from one language to the next; but this is not true.' Instead, language *differentiates* and the differences are not given in nature but issue from language itself. When we learn our native tongue, we internalise a network of distinctions that then present themselves to our consciousness as if they were there in the world.

The meanings we learn from our own language are seen as constraints but not as binding. The French can easily ascertain whether their lamb is cooked or not. I can also learn the meaning of *récuperer* as *bring into line* and turn it into an English word, or do my best to find a phrase that approximates the French. The skill of translation lies in finding near matches. And Saussure doesn't indicate that I can't distinguish degrees of intimacy because my language has only one second-person pronoun. But the implication is that what is given as natural and inevitable in the world is shaped by the language that happens to be our mother tongue. Cultural difference and linguistic difference go hand in hand.

This view has been much caricatured, most fluently by Steven Pinker in *The Blank Slate* (2002). To my mind, Pinker's target is made of straw. I do not know anyone who thinks people are blank slates inscribed only by their native language. No doubt our dispositions share much with our evolutionary ancestors, not to mention our cousins the great apes, including a propensity for signalling to one another. But the wide variety of social practices thought acceptable in the world poses a conundrum for liberal societies. From a Western perspective, it is difficult to account for cultural adherence to honour killings, female genital mutilation, child soldiers and suicide bombing. Why refuse to allow language to play a part in the construction of such different and deeply held convictions about what is right?

Oddly enough, experimental evidence is beginning to accumulate that language does influence our perception of the world at an elementary level. Vyvyan Evans lists some of it in *The Language Myth* (2014). In one instance, Greek speakers, wired up to record brain activity, were shown to register more sensitivity to different shades of blue than did English speakers. Greek divides the field of *blue* between two terms, where English doesn't. No differences between the two groups appeared in awareness of distinctions within the field of green, but then both languages have a single term for *green*.

It's not exactly a knock-down argument but it does suggest that any wholesale repudiation of Saussure has been premature. Something similar turned out to happen when Spanish speakers, whose language does not distinguish *cups* from *mugs*, were compared with English speakers for sensitivity to the shapes of drinking vessels. In a further – and perhaps more revealing – case, speakers of languages that gender sexless objects in the world were asked to characterise a range of such objects. In cases where the same thing has distinct genders in different languages, people frequently invested it with the characteristics they associated with masculinity or femininity, according to its gender in their language. For example, German speakers commonly found (feminine) bridges beautiful, elegant, fragile, slender, while Spanish speakers found the same (masculine) structures big, sturdy and towering.

Ferdinand de Saussure, 1857–1913. Professor of Linguistics at the University of Geneva. The *Course* was published after his death by his students on the basis of their lecture notes.

THE SIGNIFIER

Some would say that neuroscience and psycholinguistics have only just begun to uncover how our minds work.

Clearly, there is much more research to do. Meanwhile, Saussure's other main contribution to the story is the description of the *sign* as composed of two parts: on the one hand a *signifier* and, on the other, its meaning, or that which is *signified*. Why *signifier* in preference to *word*? Because words are not alone as bearers of meaning. In order to be inclusive in this book I have awkwardly listed as further forms of representation images and mathematical or logical symbols. In addition, gestures signify, politely or otherwise. Groups of words signify as whole phrases ('How are you?', 'Heavens to Betsy!'). Colours signify (think traffic lights). What a relief to have a single term that covers all these signifying modes, practices and objects.

But why *signifier*, not *sign*? Because the *sign* is a sign *of* something, a substitute for an object imagined as existing elsewhere, in some other form, the thing or idea as there in the world, in our heads or in the mind of God, ready and waiting to be named. *Dogs* and *cats* may seem to do that, but *phenomenology* and *the home life of hobbits* aren't meaningless because they don't. The terms bring their meanings with them.

Once the *signifier* is differentiated from the *signified*, it becomes possible to think coherently about the way meaning slips and slides. The same signifier (*crow*, *let*) may cover a range of meanings. Moreover, psychoanalysis, 'the talking cure', founded on the interpretation of speech, listens for meanings hidden even from the speaker, censored as inadmissible to consciousness but intelligible to the attentive auditor. Jacques Derrida would add that, because meaning depends on difference, not reference to the world, the trace of the repudiated differentiating term cannot be wholly excluded from the meaning of any signifier: there are no pure concepts; the other makes itself felt in the self-same, if only as something missing. No wonder Milton had difficulty in depicting good and evil as simple opposites in *Paradise Lost*; perhaps that's why he seemed to William Blake to be of the devil's party without knowing it. Consciousness itself is redoubled by the unconscious, which is not, Derrida argues, a subcutaneous hall of demons, but rather an element that is subtracted from consciousness and yet exercises an influence as what is unacknowledged or unknowable.

Jacques Derrida, 1930–2004. Professor of Philosophy in Paris and at the University of California, Irvine. He wrote over 70 books, including most notably *Of Grammatology* and *Writing and Difference* (both published in French in 1967), as well as *The Truth in Painting* (1978) and (my favourite) *The Post Card* (1980). His comments on fiction are assembled in *Acts of Literature* (1992).

He would also say that the signifier takes the place of the signified. When you speak to me, or I read Martin Amis, what I hear or see is the signifying words. I can't get behind them to a separable concept, design, or intention, try as I might. You might say more than you know; Amis might reveal unexpected meanings. I can't isolate those meanings from their formulation, however, or penetrate the signifier to get at something else. That's why some ambiguities can't be resolved but remain undecidable. But that's also why not anything goes, or why a reading I just make up ceases to be an interpretation of the text.

Language is opaque; there is nothing on the other side of it. That doesn't mean that there isn't a world or there aren't things in it. Instead, it indicates that meaning is not anchored in objects or ideas. Where the signifier matches the world, it can lead to moon landings and life-saving vaccines. Where it doesn't, it can uphold astrology, homophobia, the death camps and public beheadings, all of which have seemed to their supporters to be equally justified by a reality on the other side of the words that name it.

LANGUAGE AS CREATIVITY

The instability of meaning implies that communication does not necessarily take place. But are we still sure that communication is the project of language? There is a difference, as well as a continuity, between human and animal exchanges. Animals signal to one another in the wild: vervet monkeys utter alarm calls; bees dance to indicate where the best pollen is to be found. That is communication. But in its more developed form, language allows for dialogue, for answering back. What, then, if human language were seen instead as a place of contest – for attention, for dominance, or simply for the joy of it? How else should we account for the power of oratory or ridicule, on the one hand, and, on the other, the pleasure some people take in riddles, crosswords, charades, playing Scrabble – and writing verse, where the wits of the author are pitted against the resources of vocabulary and the rules of composition?

Either way, once we release it from its supposed moorings outside itself, language is no longer merely instrumental, there to be used as no more than a stand-in for ideas or objects. Instead, it takes its proper place as a generative force, the source of nursery rhymes, guessing games, rap, stand-up comedy, puns, undecidable ambiguities – and fiction.

'THE DEATH OF THE AUTHOR'

The opacity of writing leaves criticism no space for the author-as-explanation of the work and in 1968, the year of protest in Paris, Roland Barthes adopted the rhetoric of revolution to pronounce the author dead. Barthes's manifesto caused consternation. All over the Western world, writers rose up to declare themselves alive and well. Meanwhile, enraged critics demonstrated again and again that, even if any of them had looked beyond the title of the essay, in the event that they had so much as glanced at what Barthes had written, they had still completely missed the point. Barthes was not proposing that books wrote themselves. Instead, 'The Death of the Author' is about criticism.

Perhaps, then, the angry traditionalists had a motive for evading the issue. Appeal to the Author, the *Auteur*, originator of an *oeuvre* (Barthes gives the term a capital letter to show that the figure in question is more than just the person who does the writing) has served criticism's impulse to mastery, he argues. The accumulation of background knowledge designed to uncover the definitive secret of the work has the effect of containing the text's waywardness, its undecidability, restricting the possibilities of interpretation. 'To give a text an Author is to impose a limit on that text, to furnish it with a final signified, to close the writing.' And Barthes continues ironically: 'Such a conception suits criticism very well ... when the Author has been found, the text is "explained" – victory to the critic.'

Are works meaningless, then? Of course not. They are composed, Barthes argues, of *intertextual* traces of other works. Texts (etymologically, woven tissues, *textiles*) are drawn from 'multiple writings' and incorporate allusions and quotations; they enter into relations of exchange with other works in a process of 'dialogue, parody, contestation.' Whether or not these relations are conscious or deliberate hardly matters. The focal point of so much multiplicity is not the Author but the reader, and Barthes concludes his manifesto with a revolutionary slogan: 'the birth of the reader must be at the cost of the death of the Author'.

Roland Barthes, 1915–80. Critic and academic at the École Pratique des Hautes Études and then at the Collège de France, where he was Professor of Literary Semiology. Author most notably of *S/Z* (1970), *The Pleasure of the Text* (1975) and *A Lover's Discourse: Fragments* (1977).

From the perspective of the reader, undecidability keeps the text alive: it's why we come back to it for more. Once a text is interpreted, it's dead in our arms. But the elevation of the reader does not imply that the secret of the text slips from one head to another in a new subjectivism. This is not an idealisation of private responses; Barthes's reader is as impersonal as his Author. In the event, the addressee of the work is not an individual at all, but is 'without history, biography, psychology'. This figure is no more than the preferred destination of the text, 'simply that *someone* who holds together ... all the traces by which the written text is constituted'.

If the reign of authorial criticism is over, the time of the critic-as-reader has come, we can construe. But such criticism will demand a good deal more effort than poring over letters and diaries in the hope of uncovering in different words the single, definitive meaning of the work. Instead, interpretation will require a familiarity with as many as is humanly possible of those traces that make up the difference – the uniqueness – and the undecidability of the text.

MYTHOLOGIES

A criticism of this kind would not necessarily suspend value judgements but evaluation would not be its primary project. Nor would moral instruction. Indeed, cultural practices might be making us worse, not better. (Plato would be delighted to see that we had finally caught up with him.) The post-war question concerned not so much the lessons that literature had to teach as the myths promoted by cultures in general. Early in the *Course in General Linguistics*, Saussure had suggested the possibility of a 'science of signs' in society. Following this lead in the 1950s, Barthes wrote a series of short, witty columns about the meanings of current affairs, objects and activities. Although some of the themes have dated, even if by now *Mythologies* has been widely imitated, the irreverence and the wit can still spring surprises. Detergents, a new feature of the peacetime economy, advertise themselves as driving out dirt, rather than eliminating it: 'their function is keeping public order not making war'. Toys, now returning to the market after wartime austerity, offer an early training in docile consumerism: 'the child can only identify himself as owner, as user, never as creator; he does not invent the world, he uses it: there are, prepared for him, actions without adventure, without wonder, without joy'.

One of Barthes's observations would come to resonate strongly in the English-speaking world. A cover of *Paris Match* showed a black soldier saluting in a French uniform. His eyes are uplifted, probably fixed on the tricolour. And what does this signify? Imperialism recuperated as voluntary, gladly embraced by its subjects. At a time of mounting hostility to colonialism, the image reaffirmed the fading myth 'that France is a great Empire, that all her sons, without any colour discrimination, faithfully serve under her flag'.

Mythologies was not interested in confirming the older opposition between a demonised mass culture and life-enhancing art. On the contrary, one essay accused literature of sending to the guillotine a peasant who had no access to the literary vocabulary used in his trial. If fiction was still perceived as instilling orthodox values, that orthodoxy itself was now in question. *Mythologies* first appeared in English in 1972. By this time, identity politics had already begun to make itself felt in Anglo-American criticism. Kate Millett's *Sexual Politics* (1970) unmasked four male, broadly canonical authors from a feminist point of view. The book, witty and caustic, was an instant success, as was Germaine Greer's provocative *Female Eunuch*, published in the same year. Fiction featured prominently there, too, this time including popular romance. Postcolonial criticism was not far behind. Here the iconic work is Edward Said's *Orientalism* (1978), which also analysed a wide variety of texts to show the repeated affirmation of white superiority. Queer studies came later but is now well established – and criticism is primed either to expose oppression or to celebrate resistance as these are depicted in writings of all kinds.

The relegation of the communication model, with its author-as-sender busily transmitting univocal messages to a passive receiver, has allowed the field of criticism, its options and opportunities, to expand beyond recognition. It also promotes a new confidence that criticism has important insights to offer society. What follows from this inclusiveness deserves a new chapter.

5

WHERE NOW?

TEXTUALITY

If I had to select one work of criticism to take to a desert island (alongside the Bible and Shakespeare) it would be Roland Barthes's *S/Z* (1970). I might have chosen other books that in their day shifted the paradigm – Erich Auerbach's brilliant *Mimesis* (1953), for instance, Northrop Frye's witty *Anatomy of Criticism* (1957), or Wayne Booth's clever *Rhetoric of Fiction* (1961). But *S/Z* has probably lasted better, not least because it cannot be reduced to a single argument. The book is packed with ideas, and if one page seems unexceptional, the next can deliver a bolt from the blue. What singles out *S/Z* is its project of restoring the work to its existence as a text – to its textuality.

Like Empson's *Seven Types of Ambiguity*, *S/Z* has been slow to exert an influence on the practice of criticism. After a flurry of excitement in the 1970s, it was sidelined by other calls on our attention, some of them more given to the sweeping generalisations that proclaim a new paradigm. Like *Seven Types*, by contrast, *S/Z* requires exactly the kind of close attention it models. I choose it here because it gathers up many of the issues that have arisen in the course of this book. For one thing, *S/Z* indicates that fictional works can be coaxed to deliver more on close reading than first meets the eye, and they do so as texts in their own right, rather than as messages sent out by an author with designs on us. Value judgements are not the project of reading and, as for morality, *S/Z* is more concerned to trace the changing ethics represented in stories than to turn fiction into lessons in piety.

Barthes reads at the level of the signifier. That is to say that he does not look behind or beyond the words to find their meanings. He takes for granted that the words themselves signify but he allows for ambiguity, equivocation, the slippages that inevitably leave some meanings undecidable. To the degree that *S/Z* treats fiction as the material of a new cultural history, while recognising the romance of reading, it continues to point a way forward for criticism.

So far I have followed past critical practice in privileging poetry and drama, but *S/Z* concerns a prose work, a novella by Honoré de Balzac, reprinted at the end of Barthes's book. Balzac's *Sarrasine*, first published in 1830, is what we would now call a good read. It creates a context fascinating enough to entice a reader to want answers to the questions it sets up: who are the mysterious Lanty family? What is the source of their fabulous wealth? And who is the oddly flamboyant old man, whose emaciated appearance borders on the supernatural? Like any good realist tale, the narrative distributes hints at answers that will be confirmed only in retrospect as either clues or red herrings. In the event, the narrator in the fictional present will disclose to the woman he himself desires the past history of a sculptor, Sarrasine, who fell passionately in love with La Zambinella, a castrato singer he mistook for a woman. *S/Z: Sarrasine* divided from

Zambinella by the slash of castration. At the same time the two letters roughly mirror each other. *S/Z*: in Zambinella, Sarrasine unexpectedly contemplates his own (castrated) similitude.

Barthes classifies *Sarrasine* as *lisible*, readable (unhelpfully translated as 'readerly', which sounds like jargon). All classic works of realist fiction are readable in the ordinary sense of that term, which is to say that they have a structure, follow a logic, obey the rules of grammar. Apparently suppressing ambiguity, seemingly indifferent to paradox, they give the impression of transparency. Even though they withhold information along the way in order to delay the final disclosure, they present themselves as models of communication, placing their readers as passive receivers of the tale they tell. So clear were they thought to be that novels were latecomers to the university syllabus. What was there, after all, to challenge analysis?

At the opposite extreme of prose fiction available when *S/Z* was published in 1970 was the *nouveau roman*, designed, by rejecting all the canons of readability, to problematise the communication model. High modernism interferes with the reader's access to a well-ordered story set in a recognisable world and apparently located on the other side of the words. And it deflects in the process the illusion that the text closes on a single signified, or meaning. But Barthes posits against the readable text one that is *scriptible*, writable or (in)scribable. Such a work does not exist: it would consist of blank pages, challenging an active reader to fill the space with writing. It would therefore be completely *plural*, infinitely open to construction.

The entirely readable text, with only one single meaning, addressed to a passive consumer of its story, and the totally plural, writable one are both ideal types, purely hypothetical. Actual fiction subsists in between (deconstructing, as Jacques Derrida would put it, that opposition). The task of criticism is to be active in finding the limited plurality of any individual text, the range of meanings it can legitimately be persuaded to deliver. Nineteenth-century classic fiction presents the ultimate challenge, so sophisticated are its strategies for simulating a reality that need only be grasped for the work to be understood. What, beyond such passive recognition, can *Sarrasine* be induced to reveal? How can an active reading find what exceeds the obviousness of a communicated message?

In the first instance, where conventional criticism bypasses the signifier in favour of a generalising theme ('George Eliot gives us a cross-section of middle England') Barthes looks at the text, not through it. Nor does he seek out an overarching principle that directs the diversity of the individual signifiers towards a single purpose ('Hardy feared the effects of industrialisation on the countryside'). Such summaries, even when they result from long reflection, are necessarily reductive. The novelist Milan Kundera puts on record 'My disgust for those who reduce a work to its ideas ... My despair at this era befogged with ideas and indifferent to works'. Instead of starting with a conclusion, *S/Z* analyses the novella phrase by signifying phrase, with a view to breaking up the smooth flow of the writing. The commentary artificially slows down for inspection what we do, or might do, when we read.

Self-evidently, this is not the place to trace this process in its entirety but, as with Empson's account of ambiguity, an example may give the flavour of S/Z. Balzac's story begins innocently enough: 'I was deep in one of those daydreams which overtake even the shallowest of men, in the midst of the most tumultuous parties'. The tense implies that the events of this story belong to a past, however immediate. We are entitled to expect that they have now concluded – and we shall know how. In addition to this implicit promise of disclosure, the imperfect tense (I was daydreaming) suggests that a 'when ...' will follow, leading us to look for an interruption of the reverie, raising an expectation of the first in a sequence of actions that will constitute the story. By such devices, realism suppresses the artfulness of narration, encouraging us to look through the signifier to the events that will keep us reading to find out how they end.

Moreover, by appealing to the received wisdom, the genre invites us to recognise the reality of the world it creates: 'one of those daydreams'. Whether or not we have daydreamed at a party – and I don't think I have – the familiarity of the experience is affirmed as an obvious fact. The story puts it before us as the most natural thing in the world. Classic realism, in other words, does not always rely on a prior recognition of the world it depicts, but creates its own impression of reality, masquerading as true to a life it invents.

Meanwhile, the tumultuous party already connotes the wealth that will constitute the first enigma of the work. Connotation creates meaning without naming it: the scale of the party replaces bald statement (the hosts were rich) with the glittering substance of an occasion that also plays a part in the plot. Readable texts prefer description to abstraction, detail to generality. The project of realism, Barthes indicates, is to generate the illusion of nature, to *naturalise* what is in practice a complex and elaborate edifice.

Contrasting the noisy, social, external party with the silent, private, interior daydream, the opening sentence initiates a series of antitheses that will determine the narrative to follow: outside and inside, past and present, life and death, love and revulsion, masculine and feminine. We might add, although Barthes doesn't until later, that the intrusion of the party into the daydream will also anticipate the disruption (Derrida would say the deconstruction) of those oppositions. Most notably, the sophisticated, living present of the party will become intelligible as the outcome of a violent and deadly past, while the history of a castrato singer performing as a woman will throw into disarray not only the relationship between outside and inside, not only heterosexual romance – past and present – but also the pronouns *he* and *she*, those familiar markers of a simple antithesis between two sexes that language prompts us to take for granted.

A passive reader can choose to read for the story, taking at face value what the words denote. By contrast, Barthes's critic, as an active reader, also analyses the production of meanings on different levels. The single opening sentence, apparently no more than scene-setting, already identifies the gender of the narrator, hints at what will become the source of a mystery, and defines the components of an antithesis. Barthes compares *Sarrasine* to a polyphonic musical score where distinct instruments follow independent melodic lines at the same time.

Ideally, the critic listens to them all. As time goes on, intertextual allusions can also be heard. Early in the story, the Lantys' sixteen-year-old daughter, exotic and beautiful, is presented not in terms of a list of her physiological features but by comparison with a princess from *The Arabian Nights*. Beauty, Barthes urges, is *citational*: how, except by quoting an existing instance, can it be described? To itemise its attributes is only to fragment the body into its constituent parts, while the invocation of a familiar, purely fictional and equally unspecified beauty leaves the new one not only intact but perfect. To call the young woman as lovely as the sultan's daughter is to affirm an unassailable idea: it only seems to create an image. Later on, the narrative cites another genre: 'This mysterious family had all the appeal of one of Lord Byron's poems'. Byron's Gothic secrets help to darken Balzac's enigma, and Barthes notes ironically: 'the realistic author spends his time referring back to books: reality is what has been written'.

'ETERNAL MAN'

Reality is also whatever the proverbial wisdom acknowledges as truth. In *Sarrasine*, art is an exacting taskmaster, genius dresses badly, young people are unruly. Elsewhere in readable fiction, if uncles are not jolly, they are commonly wicked, while orphans are usually ill-treated and true love can be relied on as redemptive. Few modern works have proved more readable than the Harry Potter stories, which count on familiarity with these time-honoured verities.

Such formulae are reassuring: we know where we stand. And we recognise them from our reading, whether or not our personal experience confirms them as fact. My own stepmother, for example, might have been exceptionally loving and giving but when I come across the word in other contexts, it retains its fairy-tale frisson. Sometimes, however, the disjunction between fictional convention and current fact begins to jar and then the study of fiction can confirm that received ideas owe as much to history as they do to nature or experience. Beliefs about the world are open to change. *Sarrasine*, for example, includes the following anonymous comment on gender: 'This was woman herself, with her sudden fears, her irrational whims, her instinctive worries, her impetuous boldness, her fussings, and her delicious sensibility'.

Possibly, feminine irrationality seemed true to life in 1830; most twenty-first-century Western readers would question it now. I very much doubt whether it would have carried much conviction for Shakespeare's audiences, either: the nineteenth century was in many ways a low point for femininity. Attitudes to women, not to mention race, class and empire, are modified with time – but not always for the better.

In practice, 'woman herself' is subject to history. Without the fiction of the past to remind us otherwise, there is a temptation to suppose that what holds in our own epoch is inevitable, unalterable, the effect of human nature. It was Barthes himself in *Mythologies* who named the myth of 'Eternal Man', that figure who, since the Enlightenment, has represented us to ourselves. As the partner of woman herself, Eternal Man was originally white, as well as male, heroic, adventurous and born to rule over other races. Since his continuing role is to account for the prevailing social order, globalisation has made him slightly more ethnically diverse and less overtly domineering, but not less competitive or entrepreneurial. In the course of time, however, he has been variously rational, combative, cooperative, an individualist, sociable, acquisitive, monogamous, promiscuous, or all of the above, according to taste and political conviction.

Eternal Man rebuts the desire for change. Utopian ideals, he demonstrates, could never be made to work: 'you can't fly in the face of human nature'. Evolutionary psychology acts as one of Eternal Man's current allies: we are still at heart just hunter-gatherers; we form heterosexual pair bonds for reproduction; men pass their daylight hours at the office in order to bring home the bacon, then return to the family hearth after dark. In other words, Western suburban social conventions define not just the way things are but the way they have to be, genetically determined and hardwired into us. Social experiments, deviations from these norms, won't survive: 'it's human nature'.

Fiction complicates this image, showing a range of attitudes apparently acceptable to audiences of different epochs. Like woman herself, Eternal Man sometimes mutates. He was once aggressively territorial, but where the Roman poet Horace affirmed that 'Dulce et decorum est pro patria mori' (it is sweet and fitting to die for your country),

Wilfred Owen would echo that familiar tag with bitter irony to comment on the First World War. 'Neither a borrower nor a lender be', Shakespeare's Polonius urges his son. Sound advice in 1601, no doubt, but on that basis, a modern Laertes would never set foot on the housing ladder.

If there are certain continuities that make the fiction of the past intelligible now, times also change – and social values with them. Nothing charts these changes more accurately than fiction. Suppose we wanted to know what our predecessors made of love, conflict, mourning, revenge, friendship, hatred, we could do no better than read the stories and poems they composed about these states. Characterising such conditions is what fiction is good at. Romantic courtship has very little purchase before the twelfth century. Conversely, same-sex male friendship ranks very high in the Middle Ages, when knights needed a loyal companion who could be relied on to send for a surgeon. The revenge ethic came into serious question in sixteenth-century England, as the state set out to take control of private quarrels. Family values peaked in the nineteenth century; war lost much of its lustre in 1914–18.

Fiction shows how conceptions of virtue and villainy alter over time. In order to trace such changes we should need to overcome the temptation to think that, whatever they wrote, storytellers must *really* have understood these qualities exactly as we do. But if we succeeded in that, we might (I'll venture to say would) find a degree of relativity proving that change is not only possible but inevitable, kept in check only by inertia – as well as the myths of both woman herself and Eternal Man.

As I indicated in chapter 3, historicism old and New has largely confined itself to studying the background in order to explain the fiction. But what if we reversed the process? Suppose, in other words, we treated fiction as a source of cultural history? Fiction depicts what passes at any time for good or evil, glorious or shameful; it defines what prompts desire or aversion. Oddly enough, this is not a new idea. Here is John Morley, eminent Liberal Statesman and General Editor of the English Men of Letters series, commenting in 1887 on the value of studying fiction:

> My notion of the literary student is one who through books explores the strange voyages of man's moral reason, the impulses of the human heart, the chances and changes that have overtaken human ideals of virtue and happiness, of conduct and manners, and the shifting fortunes of great conceptions of truth and virtues.

Fiction promotes the study of fluctuating values in history. It's not a bad programme.

EQUIVOCATION

Would this study centre, then, on extracting the commonplaces and stereotypes from works of different epochs? Not exactly. Let's go back to the quotation from *Sarrasine*. It will turn out, although neither the hero nor the reader yet knows it for sure, that the subject of the comment on woman herself, with her timid and irrational fussings, is not a woman at all, but a female impersonator. Can we, in those circumstances, take the pronouncement to have passed for truth at the time?

As an instance of free, indirect discourse, the observation has no source, no inverted commas, no 'he thought', no evident origin. Who, then, is telling us that this is the essence of femininity? Balzac, drawing on his knowledge of women? Balzac commenting ironically on what passes for feminine in his society? Sarrasine, convinced that the figure he loves is a woman? Sarrasine, persuading himself that the figure he loves is a woman, despite a growing doubt? The novella itself, reassuring the reader, in order to postpone the crucial disclosure? Or perhaps the novella inviting the reader to collude with it in perceiving Sarrasine's self-deception?

The story doesn't say. Readers may choose one view or another but criticism cannot legitimately settle for any one of these readings at the expense of the others. Neither can it finally resolve the question of whether this characterisation of woman is offered as a truth that would understandably confirm Sarrasine's view, along with the nineteenth-century reader's (women are indeed timid and instinctive), or an irony that distances readers from Sarrasine (he is reaching for the cliché that women are timid and instinctive).

How, then, can we hope to derive a history of values from fiction, if undecidability is back in a new guise, obscuring the process of communication? This time, ambiguity does not present itself as a single word or phrase with more than one meaning, but takes the form of equivocation, which conceals while it seems to reveal. Withholding its own status as truth or falsehood, the comment on woman only pretends to communicate. In practice, it introduces uncertainty in the interests of the story. The maintenance of the enigma (who in the past was Sarrasine's beloved? who now is the little old man?) depends on withholding the gender of the castrato in the guise of a woman. Read ironically as a false account of women, the sentence constitutes a clue to the truth about its subject, the castrato; taken straight, it lies about the castrato, while offering to tell the truth about women.

Nor is this an isolated instance of narrative equivocation. Every time the castrato is identified by a pronoun, the story faces a choice. 'He' would give the game away, destroying the suspense that holds our attention; 'she' misleads. Given Saussure's emphasis on the difficulty of translation, it is worth noting that in this respect *Sarrasine* presents any number of riddles for the translator. When it comes to pronouns, French has an advantage that English lacks. The gender of the possessive pronoun in French agrees with the following noun, not with the possessor. In consequence, the French narrative can avoid committing itself to the sex of the singer in some of the cases where English makes a decision necessary: 'son protecteur' (her – or his – protector); 'sa poitrine' (her bosom or his chest). Elsewhere, however, English remains uncommitted where the French can only either mislead or spoil the surprise: 'je serai forcée' (feminine) (I shall be forced).

While in this instance it is pronouns that constitute a major obstacle to communication, other kinds of prevarication recur in all readable texts. For the sake of the plot, to preserve the surprise that attends the final disclosure, we are regularly incited to misread, pointed in the direction of the wrong murderer, led to favour the wrong suitor or misconstrue the right one. Classic realist writing only appears transparent, while veiling the truth for the duration. Barthes calls this inevitable equivocation a 'defect in communication'.

A SUBTLER CULTURAL HISTORY

But surely, everything is made clear at the end of the story, when Sarrasine's tragic error is disclosed? In crime fiction the murderer is revealed; romances show where true love belongs; Mr Wickham is exposed for what he is and Mr Darcy vindicated. Readable fiction promises that we shall be able to look back through the story and see where it misled us. Such disclosure is not always complete, however, and some ambiguities remain. The status of our sentence about woman herself with her fussings remains undecidable. The three possibilities remain in place. Is it, first, offered as a true observation on women, mistakenly applied by Sarrasine to a castrato? Second, are we to see it as a true observation misleadingly applied by the narrator to a castrato? Or is it, finally, an irony apparent to a perceptive reader – or on a second reading – and false in its entirety?

In practice, a cultural history derived from fiction would not rely on a single sentence in isolation from its context in the work. How, then, does *Sarrasine* depict its women characters? Are they, too, timorous and excitable, in confirmation of the comment? According to Barthes's analysis, they feature as surprisingly powerful: he calls them castrators; it is the men, he notes, who turn out to be ineffectual. Does the rest of the novella instead dispel the view that in 1830 women are perceived as timid, intuitive and irrational?

Yes and no. The power exercised by the women in the story is artful, discreet, manipulative; it is maintained without sacrificing what passes for feminine conduct. A third interpretation, then, begins to suggest itself: women at this time generally act to some degree as female impersonators; they hold considerable power by subscribing to the socially recognised idea of woman, representing themselves as feminine, timid, irrational. They wield their diffidence like a weapon in the war between the sexes. In other words, what passes for femininity is no more than a performance.

No one of these readings of the sentence from *Sarrasine* offers itself as definitive. If the observation is to serve the interests of the story in its immediate context, postponing the final disclosure, the view that women fuss must be at least plausible in 1830. As prevarication, however, it is open, at least in retrospect, to ironic interpretation. And finally, if we place the comment in relation to the depiction of women in the novella, we cannot exclude the third possibility, that 'woman herself' relies, paradoxically, on an impersonation of what is seen as feminine. If so, in *Sarrasine*, while realist fiction only masquerades as truth, while the prevailing beliefs only masquerade as nature, femininity itself is no more than a masquerade. The dance that connotes the wealth of the Lanty family also stands as an emblem of a realm of dazzling surfaces and seductive outward display.

A cultural history based on fiction would do justice to these competing possibilities, paying close attention to equivocation. And in the process it would produce a subtler and more complex story of changing values. At this moment in French history, we can say on the basis of *Sarrasine*, relations between the sexes were a source of anxiety. Women, it would seem, were officially idealised, pitied or disparaged, the real threat they were held to represent masked by either over-valuation or contempt.

But couldn't we reduce all this to evidence of Balzac's personal problem with women? Not if we take account of his success with the reading public. 'The Death of the Author' put the reader at the heart of criticism for a reason. From the point of view of a historian of culture, the question is not what drives authors so much as what engages readers, not what went on privately in the mind of an individual writer, but what drew the attention of the public to the text. The widespread revival of interest in *Sarrasine* in the 1960s that Barthes mentions surely marked another moment of instability in gender relations, when a resurgent feminism was ready to form a tentative alliance with the campaign to legalise homosexuality. Our pronouns, it now began to appear, had indeed misled us: sexual difference was no longer simply binary. A story concerning transgender identity became a source of fascination, though without erasing the horror of a historic violence, castration, once practised in the name of art.

CULTURAL CRITICISM

That initial violence is also central to Balzac's story as the secret source of the Lanty fortune. If *Sarrasine* casts an ambiguous light on past attitudes to gender, it also illuminates the complex history of money. The wealth of the Lantys, visible in the resplendent social gathering, is in practice earned by a castrato singer and therefore bloodstained, secret because inadmissible. But how far, the cultural historian might ask, can there ever be innocent wealth? How much do vast fortunes necessarily owe to the past appropriation of land, or labour, or sex?

And now? If money as banknotes, as plastic, suppresses its own origins, if our own violence is practised figuratively in boardrooms as well as literally in backstreets, one person's gain still entails another person's loss. These issues reappear in contemporary fiction, not only in Oliver Stone's *Wall Street* (1987), Don DeLillo's *Cosmopolis* (2003) or John Lanchester's *Capital* (2012) but also in soap opera whenever it tackles disparities of income and the experience of poverty. Cultural criticism, attentive to the present as well as the past history of values, looks to fiction as one source of information about current concerns and convictions. How does our own society, or our community, assess luxury and hardship?

How, come to that, does it understand the emotions of love, grief, friendship, hate? What does it make of sex and sexual identity? Fiction continues to find ways of defining and redefining conditions and feelings that are hard to talk about, not least because they themselves are often ambiguous, or equivocate with us, masquerading as other than they are. One task for criticism is attention to their changing depiction in the stories that circulate now.

On the evidence, it won't be easy. The texts require the closest attention to their own ambiguities and equivocations, their evasions as well as their affirmations. Cultural criticism finds that the received ideas of the twenty-first century are as complex and as contradictory as those held in the past. Our values are evident in the meanings fiction puts forward, but those meanings often remain uncertain, undecidable.

Undecidability between clearly defined options is neither nebulous nor vague, however. As *S/Z* demonstrates, reading for equivocation has nothing to do with making up interpretations to suit our own preferences. And it's surely worth the effort. Criticism encourages us to stand back from competing current versions of the received wisdom and reassess the values that contemporary culture takes for granted, aspires to or rejects. If, as current theory suggests, culture plays a part in shaping our view of the world, and if culture resides above all in the meanings we share and contest, the analysis of current fiction allows us a critical take on our own attitudes and values.

But it can do this only on condition that we reunite the two halves of our source material, now divided institutionally between English on the one hand, selective and mainly historical, and cultural studies on the other, popular and largely contemporary. There is no possibility of understanding current social values without reference to popular culture. Conversely, an analysis that ignores independent cinema, experimental theatre or so-called literary fiction is hobbled from the start by its own populism. New and difficult work can reach previously uncharted territory, just as blockbusters may succeed to the degree that they reaffirm – or break with – the existing formula. And if we cannot usefully isolate one branch of culture from another, neither can we afford to emphasise the present at the expense of history. Contemporary culture is best understood in its continuities with and differences from the social values that have prevailed in the past. If we are to understand ourselves, and the contribution of culture to shaping the people we are, we need to be willing to engage with that culture, past and present, in its entirety.

THE CURRICULUM

When it comes to education, if I had my way children would be encouraged to associate reading with enjoyment from the earliest possible age. In selecting the material for use in class, I would put the emphasis not so much on inculcating whatever passes with orthodoxy for virtue, but more, in line with Gray, Matthew Arnold and the Newbolt Committee, on expanding vocabulary. New words bring new ideas to think with. I would also – and this will not be popular in many official quarters – teach grammar, if only to show how much linguistic exchange owes to convention: syntax connects thoughts in specific ways, for better or worse. Whatever you might want to say, the order of the words will affect what people make of it. The so-called rules of grammar are not guaranteed from some elevated place outside language itself; on the contrary, they are there to be broken, but not before their implications have been grasped.

I would give all children access to at least one second language, so that they could see for themselves how distinct cultures arrange the world in different ways. And at the earliest possible opportunity I would invite students to see meaning as unfixed and equivocal. Whether at the level of words and phrases or of whole texts, signifying practices are not 'subjective', not at the disposal of the individual, not their personal property. But meaning is not owned by anyone else either, and so cannot be subject to univocal definition by authority. I would, in consequence, treat the English lesson as a place to challenge linguistic and critical fundamentalisms.

From there it should be easy enough to embark in due course on a programme of cultural criticism, where students become active critics. The young have an investment in their own culture, not least in its difference from the values of the past. We could take that as a starting point – but not stop there. How far, we could go on to ask, are Romeo and Juliet like us? And who, in that context, do we mean by 'us'? Current Western societies include communities loyal to the idea of arranged marriage. In addition, how are Shakespeare's lovers different? Let's not pretend romantic love has no history or that the lapse of four centuries changes nothing. I would put difference at the heart of all education in the humanities.

THE ROMANCE OF READING

Meanwhile, fiction gives pleasure. Cultural criticism offers intellectual insights into our conception of the world on the grounds that its material has such widespread appeal. It is because it attracts readers and audiences that fiction provides access to social values in their continuity and difference. That the work was written shows what was imaginable at the time; that it was read implies that what was imagined also resonated with others. There are many possible motives for reading: to keep up, to belong, to impress. But beyond all these, and more powerful by far, is enjoyment.

As far as we know, there are no cultures without stories and songs, whether these take the form of myths, news, fireside tales, dramatic performances, epics, novels and films, on the one hand, or, on the other, chants, hymns, nursery rhymes, work songs, lyrics and odes. Fiction offers to enlist our sympathies in heroism, revenge and forgiveness, magic, the sacred, desire and grief. All the evidence indicates that people – not everyone, for sure, but enough to count – seem to relish this engagement of their feelings within the safe space marked out by the signifier. Words and images make passions live; at the same time, they contain the intensities they bring to light ('it's only a story').

Even so, the emotions that fiction is capable of arousing may be strong enough to enthral. Reading can be akin to romance, while listeners sometimes develop a special relationship with storytellers. Desdemona fell in love with Othello when he recounted his life history, he tells the Venetian senate – a tale of battles won and lost and narrow escapes in wild places, as well as wonders unknown in sixteenth-century Venice. When this account drew Desdemona from her household tasks to hear more, it was narrative itself that enlisted her desire – and she dropped Othello a large hint, he reports:

> She thanked me
> And bade me, if I had a friend that loved her,
> I should but teach him how to tell my story
> And that would woo her.

The Duke is not surprised to hear it: 'I think this tale would win my daughter too'.

Desdemona was not the first woman to be captivated by a narrative, however. As Shakespeare would have known, it was while Aeneas related the tragic history of the fall of Troy that Dido gave her heart to the exiled hero. Nor is it only women who are susceptible to tales. Shahrazad succeeds in postponing her execution for 1001 nights by the stories she tells the king until, in the end, he marries this skilful weaver of fictions and makes her his queen. 'At the origin of Narrative, desire', Barthes comments succinctly. No wonder the first-person narrator of Sarrasine's history expects a romantic response from the marquise who so longs to hear it: 'a night of love for a good story'.

As the *Arabian Nights* suggests, suspense plays a part in the appeal of a well-told tale. Shahrazad prolongs her life by the device that in due course magazine fiction and TV series will also use to maintain their audiences. Each night, she leaves the tale incomplete, or begins a new one, so that the king keeps her alive to find out how the story ends. While the enigmas remain unresolved, while closure is withheld, we are motivated to listen, watch or read on.

But suspense is not, in my view, the whole explanation, or we should never reread the same story. People return again and again to *Emma* and *Jane Eyre*; staged versions of familiar films currently fill theatres. If guessing the ending were the only motive, playgoers would not be drawn to new productions of Shakespeare when they've seen earlier versions. Dido asks Aeneas to recount the fall of Troy, already knowing exactly how it will end. Desdemona can see that Othello has survived his daring escapades, or he would not be here to tell the tale. What's more, although lyrics and sonnets sometimes rely on an element of narrative, they rarely involve suspense. In 'A slumber did my spirit seal', to return for a moment to Wordsworth's elegiac poem, the event is over; the enigma, if there is one, does not concern what took place. Instead, the lyric centres on an irretrievable loss. So, in its way, does the story Aeneas tells Dido.

'At the origin of Narrative, desire.'

What she implicitly wants to hear, what moves her in the telling, is the account of what it was like to be there. My guess is that how it feels matters as much as what happens.

THE TALE, NOT THE TELLER

Sarrasine's narrator, who hopes for a night of love in exchange for his story, will in the event be disappointed. Repelled by the history of a fortune based on castration, the marquise turns away from the storyteller and is left deep in thought. Aeneas and Othello initially fare better, but if Shahrazad and the king live happily ever after, both Dido and Desdemona will come to an unhappy end at the hands of their lovers.

What price, then, the romance of reading if it's dangerous to fall in love with authors? But perhaps the author only stands in for something else, however improbable that something might appear. William Stoner, for one, finds a more consistent object of desire. In the second year of his degree course in agriculture, designed to return him better qualified to help his parents on their farm, the protagonist of *Stoner* is required to pursue a survey course in English Literature. When the lecturer reads out Shakespeare's Sonnet 73, 'That time of year thou mayst in me behold', and asks the student to comment, he can only stutter. The unassuming Stoner finds no words to speak about the poem – but not out of ignorance or indifference. On the contrary, after the class is dismissed, 'he sat unmoving, staring out before him at the narrow planked flooring that had been worn bare of varnish by the restless feet of students he would never see or know'. Eventually, he too leaves the room, newly aware of the 'bare gnarled branches of the trees that curled and twisted against the pale sky' in an echo of Shakespeare's 'bare ruined choirs where late the sweet birds sang'. The following semester, he switches to English.

John Williams's *Stoner*, first published in 1965 and reissued in 2003, traces the inner life of a dedicated teacher of English. The encounter with Sonnet 73 remakes his world, so that a deeply felt emotion he finds it hard to name invests familiar objects with new vividness. Stoner has fallen in love, but with a poem. His subsequent story is not a happy one and his human relationships fail one by one. Through all the vicissitudes of his life, however, he remains faithful to that single passion for Renaissance poetry.

What is there to add? In my view, a major task that now faces criticism is to account for the romance of reading, the curious compulsion exercised by stories and poems. For all our critical sophistication, despite our range of approaches and methods, we have barely begun to answer that crucial question. What in them draws us to stories and lyrics? What feature or features of fiction enlist our desire?

We know something about language and the part it plays in shaping identity. We are also beginning to recognise that other animals, too, experience such feelings as attachment, fear and grief. But they don't, apparently, exchange accounts of them or investigate what they mean. Fiction does. It seeks a vocabulary that goes to the heart of what it is to be a signifying human animal, subjected, in consequence, to all the temporal continuity and cultural difference that the human condition entails. Criticism will realise its potential when it finds a way of doing justice to the special engagement that fiction generates with its representation of changing ideals, ambivalent allegiances and passions to be found at the limits of language.

That, at least, is my view. But what do you think?

ILLUSTRATIONS

Page 13: The engraved title page of Thomas Percy's *Reliques* (1765). (Cambridge University Library)

Page 36: Kristin Scott Thomas as Sophocles's *Electra*, 2015. (© Johan Persson/ArenaPAL)

Page 52: Detail from Leonardo da Vinci's *Mona Lisa*. (Louvre Museum: © Dennis Hallinan/Alamy Stock Photo)

Page 63: Edward Henry Lamson, *A Country Schoolroom*, 1890. (Yale University Art Gallery)

Page 91: Woodcut by Agnes Miller Parker from Thomas Gray, *Elegy Written in a Country Churchyard* (London: Raven Press, 1938) (facing verse 13). (Cambridge University Library)

Page 141: Detail from Iranian book cover, early nineteenth century. (© Trustees of the British Museum)

REFERENCES

CHAPTER 1

Wordsworth's 'A slumber did my spirit seal' is widely anthologised. To locate the poem in its original setting, along with the Preface, see Fiona Stafford, ed., *Lyrical Ballads, 1798 and 1802* (Oxford: Oxford University Press, 2013).

Valentine comments on Silvia in *Two Gentlemen of Verona* (2.1.5), and Miranda on Ferdinand in *The Tempest* (1.2.417–19). (Shakespeare references may vary from one edition to another.)

'Let me be what I am' is in Ben Jonson, *The Complete Poems*, George Parfitt, ed. (Harmondsworth: Penguin, 1975), pp. 179–81.

For 'The unquiet grave' see F. J. Child, *The English and Scottish Popular Ballads*, 78 A.

'Upon her feet' can be found in *The Complete Poetry of Robert Herrick*, Tom Cain and Ruth Connolly, eds (Oxford: Oxford University Press, 2013), 2 vols, vol. 1, p. 183.

Coleridge's comment appears in Earl Leslie Griggs, ed., *The*

Collected Letters of Samuel Taylor Coleridge (Oxford: Clarendon Press, 1956), vol. 1, pp. 479–80.

Harold Bloom, as one prominent example, treats Margaret Hutchinson as the theme of the poem in *How to Read and Why* (London: Fourth Estate, 2000), pp. 121–2.

J. Hillis Miller's analysis is reprinted as 'On Edge: The Crossways of Contemporary Criticism' in *Romanticism and Contemporary Criticism*, Morris Eaves and Michael Fischer, eds (Ithaca, NY: Cornell University Press, 1986), pp. 96–126. I have referred to pp. 106–7.

William Empson drew attention to the urgent need for good sense in *Seven Types of Ambiguity* (London: Chatto and Windus, 1953), p. 123.

CHAPTER 2

Simon Forman's reports are reproduced in the Arden editions of *Macbeth* (London: Bloomsbury, 2015), pp. 337–8, and *The Winter's Tale* (London: A & C Black, 2010), pp. 84–5.

Plato discusses fiction in *The Republic* when he considers education (376c–403c) as well as the theory of art (595a–608b). The text is available in a range of modern translations, as is Aristotle's *Poetics* (also known as *The Art of Poetry*), where the single paragraph defining tragedy that has given rise to so much debate is in section 49b.

For the quotations from Shelley's *Defence of Poetry*, see *Percy Bysshe Shelley: The Major Works*, Zachary Leader and Michael O'Neill, eds (Oxford: Oxford University Press, 2003), pp. 674–701, esp. p. 701.

I have quoted Matthew Arnold, *Reports on Elementary Schools* (London: Macmillan, 1908), pp. 228–9.

Horace's *Art of Poetry* is also known as *Epistle to the Pisos*. More than one modern translation is available in paperback, including Horace, *Satires and Epistles* (Oxford: Oxford University Press, 2011), pp. 106–18.

Alexander Pope's *Essay on Criticism* is readily available. I have quoted lines 715–16, 89, 298 and 233–4.

Boccaccio's *Life of Dante* exists in a range of translations. I used the version published by Garland (New York, 1990).

The story of the apparition can be found in Izaak Walton, *Lives of John Donne, Sir Henry Wotton, Richard Hooker, George Herbert and Robert Sanderson* (London: Falcon Educational Books, 1951), pp. 21–6.

For *Leonardo da Vinci and a Memory of his Childhood* see Sigmund Freud, *Art and Literature* (London: Penguin, 1985), pp. 143–231; the smile is discussed on pp. 199–205. The fully revised version of Ernest Jones's account of *Hamlet and Oedipus* was published in London by Victor Gollancz (1949).

Milan Kundera comments on biography in *The Art of the Novel* (London: Faber and Faber, 2005), p. 146.

For the observation of Friedrich Nietzsche that I have singled out, see *The Birth of Tragedy* (London: Penguin, 2003), p. 40.

For Jacques Lacan's theory of culture's magic circle, see Catherine Belsey, *Culture and the Real* (London: Routledge, 2005).

CHAPTER 3

Shakespeare's Arion appears in *Twelfth Night*, 1.2.14; Prospero rejects magic in *The Tempest*, 5.1.33–57. The players are rallied in *Hamlet*, 3.2.1–45; Brutus addresses the Romans in *Julius Caesar*, 3.2.13–34.

For documents on Victorian education, including Minnie Bulmer's exercise book (pp. 240–44), see Anne Digby and Peter Searby, *Children, School and Society in Nineteenth-Century England* (London: Macmillan, 1981). The Newbolt Report is available online at http://www.educationengland. org.uk/documents/newbolt/newbolt1921.html

The national curriculum for the teaching of English in England 2014 can be found at https://www.gov.uk/ government/publications/national-curriculum-in-england-english- programmes-of-study

Matthew Arnold, 'The Study of Poetry', first published in 1880 and included in his *Essays in Criticism: Second Series* (1888), is widely anthologised. I have quoted from the opening paragraphs. *Culture and Anarchy* (1869, available in paperback from Oxford University Press, 2009) displays Arnold's rejection of conventional piety in favour of an openness to new ideas.

The emergence of English as a university subject is traced by D. J. Palmer in *The Rise of English Studies* (London: Oxford University Press, 1965) and Chris Baldick, *The Social Mission of English Criticism, 1848–1932* (Oxford: Clarendon Press, 1983).

Leavis is easily readable. For a commentary on his work and its implications, see Francis Mulhern, *The Moment of Scrutiny* (London: New Left Books, 1979).

Martha C. Nussbaum makes the case for literature in *Not for Profit: Why Democracy Needs the Humanities* (Princeton, NJ: Princeton University Press, 2010).

The flowers lament their lost chastity at *A Midsummer Night's Dream*, 3.1.193.

I have quoted Raymond Williams, *Culture and Society* (Harmondsworth: Penguin, 1963), p. 304.

CHAPTER 4

Gray's 'Elegy Written in a Country Churchyard' was an immediate success and has been widely anthologised ever since.

Robert Graves and Laura Riding, *A Survey of Modernist Poetry* is available in a modern edition by Charles Mundye and Patrick McGuinness (Manchester: Carcanet, 2002). I have quoted p. 38.

I have cited the third edition of *Seven Types of Ambiguity* (1953). *Macbeth* features on pp. 18–20 and 82. Empson's extract from the play is 3.2.47–54. The quotation from *Hamlet* is at 1.4.85.

I have quoted Pope's *Essay on Man*, Epistle 2, line 18. The Henry Vaughan lines are from the final verse of 'The Night'.

Cleanth Brooks cites *Macbeth*, 1.7.21–3. I have quoted his essay, 'The Naked Babe and the Cloak of Manliness', *The Well Wrought Urn* (London: Denis Dobson, 1968), pp. 17–39, esp. p. 38.

'The Intentional Fallacy' can be found in W. K. Wimsatt, *The Verbal Icon* (London: Methuen, 1970), pp. 3–18. I have quoted pp. 5 and 10.

Ferdinand de Saussure, *Course in General Linguistics* (London: Fontana, 1974) is translated by Wade Baskin.

Beware of other translations, which lead to confusion when they eschew the English terms that are now current. I have quoted p. 116. The proposal for a science of signs is on p. 16.

Vyvyan Evans lists evidence for the influence of language on perception in *The Language Myth* (Cambridge: Cambridge University Press, 2014), pp. 192–228.

'The Death of the Author' is available in Roland Barthes, *Image – Music – Text* (London: Fontana, 1977), pp. 142–8. I have quoted pp. 147 and 148.

From Roland Barthes, *Mythologies* (London: Vintage, 2009) I have quoted pp. 32, 58, 139.

CHAPTER 5

Roland Barthes, *S/Z* (London: Cape, 1975, reissued Oxford: Basil Blackwell, 1990). I have quoted pp. 17–18, 33–4, 39, 172–3, 145, 88, 89. Barthes also quotes the comment on 'woman herself' in the opening sentence of 'The Death of the Author' (p. 142). Eternal Man features in *Mythologies*, p. 167.

Milan Kundera makes his observation in *The Art of the Novel*, p. 131.

The Latin quotation is from Ode III.2.13, translated in Horace, *The Complete Odes and Epodes* (Oxford: Oxford

University Press, 1997); Wilfred Owen's 'Dulce et decorum est' is widely anthologised. Polonius advises Laertes in *Hamlet*, 1.3.75.

John Morley is quoted in Palmer, *The Rise of English Studies*, p. 93.

The hero describes the effect of his life story in *Othello*, 1.3.129–70. Aeneas recounts the fall of Troy in Virgil, *Aeneid*, Books 2 and 3. (Translations are widely available.)

The student's reaction to the Shakespeare sonnet can be found in John Williams, *Stoner* (London: Vintage, 2003), pp. 10–13.

I discuss the romance of reading in *A Future for Criticism* (Oxford: Wiley-Blackwell, 2011), especially chapters 1 and 7.

FURTHER READING

GENERAL

In addition to those I have discussed, the following works of twentieth-century criticism, whether or not we would agree with them now, have exercised a major influence and significantly altered the critical landscape. Erich Auerbach, *Mimesis* (Princeton NJ: Princeton University Press, 1953) traces the emergence of realism in close readings of passages of European fiction from Homer to Virginia Woolf. Northrop Frye, *Anatomy of Criticism* (Princeton NJ: Princeton University Press, 1957) offers a structuralist classification of works according to type. Wayne C. Booth, *The Rhetoric of Fiction* (Chicago IL: University of Chicago Press, 1961) is the source, among other concepts, of 'the unreliable narrator'. Gérard Genette, *Narrative Discourse* (Oxford: Blackwell, 1980) provides a vocabulary for the textual analysis of the novel.

Alternatively, if you are tempted by a quantitative approach, try Franco Moretti, 'The Slaughterhouse of Literature', 'Planet Hollywood' and 'Network Theory, Plot Analysis', *Distant Reading* (London: Verso, 2013), pp. 63–89, 91–105, 211–40. In *Loving Literature: A Cultural History* (Chicago IL: University of Chicago Press, 2015), Deirdre Shauna Lynch challenges the view that criticism and theory lead to a joyless desiccation of our favourite books, and charts a complicated love affair with fiction in the century between 1750 and 1850 that still smoulders in classrooms today.

PRACTITIONERS

Some of the best critics have been writers. For the impersonality of poetry, see T. S. Eliot, 'Tradition and the Individual Talent', *Selected Essays* (London: Faber and Faber, 1951), pp. 13–22. As a practising dramatist, Berthold Brecht constantly returned to the relationship between the play and the audience. How could they be persuaded to sit up and take notice? See *Brecht on Theatre*, John Willett, trans. (London: Eyre Methuen, 1964). For stimulus it would be hard to beat Milan Kundera, *The Art of the Novel* (London: Faber and Faber, 2005); Toni Morrison, *Playing in the Dark: Whiteness and the Literary Imagination* (London: Picador, 1993); and Margaret Atwood, *On Writers and Writing* (London: Virago, 2015).

FRENCH THEORY

There is much more to be said on this topic. I discuss its implications for fiction in more detail in *Critical Practice* (London: Routledge, 2002) and *Poststructuralism: A Very Short Introduction* (Oxford: Oxford University Press, 2002). But there is no substitute for the real thing. In addition to the works I have discussed in the course of this book, try first Jacques Derrida, *Monolingualism of the Other* (Stanford, CA: Stanford University Press, 1998). Derek Attridge has assembled Derrida's commentaries on fiction in *Acts of Literature* (New York: Routledge, 1992). Roland Barthes, *A Lover's Discourse: Fragments* is a delight to read (London: Jonathan Cape, 1979). Michel Foucault, *The History of Sexuality* (London: Allen Lane, 1979) radically redefined the history of sexual identities. Shoshana Felman, 'Turning the Screw of Interpretation' made me rethink Henry James – and everything else: see *Literature and Psychoanalysis*, Shoshana Felman, ed. (Baltimore, MD: Johns Hopkins University Press, 1982), pp. 94–2.

INDEX